The Yellow Star That Wasn't

Scandinavia, Miami, and Me

Wartime Jews in Scandinavia From Helsinki to a Miami Beach Obsession

Cami Ann Green

Award-Winning Author of Human Interest Stories

The Yellow Star That Wasn't

Copyright © 2020 by Cami Ann Green

For information contact :
Cami Ann Green
http://www.CHofstadter.com

Book and Cover design by Seagreen Press, LLC
ISBN: 978-0-9882169-2-1

First Edition: November, 2020

TABLE OF CONTENTS

A FEW NOTES FOR THE READER

Although it may seem like the title of this book (*… and Me*) should put it squarely in the genre of memoirs, I consider it a *hybrid* as it combines the historical facts of what happened to the wartime Jews in Scandinavia with my journey from Helsinki, Finland, where I grew up as a postwar, Protestant, Swedish-speaking girl living a life of illusion. The yearning to find a place to fit in has since taken me to Miami, Florida, the place where I first learned the truth about the King of Denmark and his Yellow Star.

In the words of Oliver Sacks, the famed neurologist and author, the human race is all about stories. Through them, we learn to understand ourselves and how to relate to each other. In the case of this book, the unusual anecdotes and turns of events, based in the later research I did to prepare for my talks about the fate of the wartime Jews in Scandinavia, also serve the purpose of teaching a multifaceted slice of history without overloading the reader with facts and statistics that'd only detract from the learning experience.

While the facts are true throughout the text, the imagined speech of the characters is an artistic device by authors of creative non-fiction (memoir). Unless equipped with a recorder, writers can only write about their own recollection or understanding of dialogues. Here, I may have an added advantage in that I'm a lifelong diarist who frequently penned exact details of verbal exchanges.

The geographic area requires a brief explanation. An observant reader may notice that Iceland isn't included in what I alternatively call *Scandinavia* or the *Nordic countries* (although, historically, the two aren't the same). This is because that island-nation didn't gain its independence from Denmark until 1944.

For any writer, style can be a dilemma. For me, the form for antisemitism was at first a problem: lower or upper case, hyphen or no hyphen? Should I let the correction feature of my word processing program dictate style, since it was so insistent on its own changes? For a variety of philosophical reasons, eloquently expressed by others, I finally decided to follow the usage by respected scholars: *antisemitism*.

As a reader of other languages than English (including Danish, Finnish, Norwegian, and Swedish), I also faced the conundrum of the format for what the Nazis called the *Judenfrage*. While it's one word in German (and Swedish, for that matter), it's alternatively written in English with an upper or lower case for what then becomes the two-word term of Jewish Question or question. Since I found no consistency in my sources, including the website of Yad Vashem, I settled on the capitalized style.

Finally, although "Andy" was a very real person in my life, I've changed his name here, as I did with all identifying characteristics of him and his family. Any resemblance to another person is purely coincidental.

Cami Ann Green

Miami, Florida
November, 2020

PROLOGUE

IN JANUARY 2000, amid man-sized piles of snow in Moscow, the Russian capital, I trudge up the steps to a brand-new activity center for Jewish seniors. Although I'm living in Miami, Florida, a friend has arranged for me and my fiancée, Andy, to be part of an eight-person delegation from the New York Joint Distribution Committee, a Jewish humanitarian assistance organization founded in 1914. It seems the rest of the group, all Jewish except me, hasn't made any special preparations for the visit either so I decide to just hang back and observe. On the way to the facility there'd been an animated discussion about how to communicate with the people we'll visit, all members of a generation that usually doesn't know any English. None of us speaks Russian.

When one of the ladies says she knows a little Yiddish, rusty as it is since her parents passed away long ago, there's a communal sigh of relief. We have our default leader.

We're greeted by a group of perhaps thirty administrators and day residents, all of whom are visibly thrilled to show us, the *amerikanskiy*, the new building. We peek at tables set up with board- and card-games we don't recognize, we admire unfamiliar supplies lining open cabinet shelves, and we cluck over primitive craft projects. At the end of our tour, our hosts pour tea from a traditional *samovar* and hand us cookies on plastic plates festooned with a tiny white paper napkin so shiny and stiff that it doesn't even absorb a drop of liquid.

Our spokesperson, the only one in our group who can spout social niceties in Yiddish, makes an announcement. Now it's their turn to ask questions of us, she says with an inviting smile. And, for extra emphasis, " *fregn, fregn*; ask, ask."

There's an instant commotion among the men and women sitting on flimsy folding chairs along the edges of the room. Gesticulating to each other, they chatter in incomprehensible Russian. Finally, one lady, stout and in a drab well-worn blue dress, stands up.

Wagging her right index finger pointedly in my direction across the room, she calls out in Yiddish, "*Iz zi idishe?*" (is she Jewish?).

Without thinking, I shout across the room in my best German, "*Nein, ich komme aus Finnland. In Helsinki geboren*" (No, I come from Finland. Born in Helsinki). As if being from Finland precludes one from being Jewish.

But the *babushka* isn't taken back. She breaks into a big smile and, with an unexpectedly steady gait, scampers across the floor, throws her arms around me and plants kisses all over my face. For the rest of our visit she doesn't let go of my hand. The love between the Russian and Finnish people, Jews and Gentiles alike, runs irrevocably deep, in spite of a long history of wars and political strife.

Still, the sudden embarrassment from my uncharacteristic impulsiveness makes me wince. Had I really forgotten the voice of my forefathers with their still-prevailing social norms of never setting oneself apart in any way? Hadn't I learned anything from my mother's enduring admonishment – *don't think you're special* – that still rings in my ears, even now, decades after I left Helsinki for Miami?

Part 1
Yellow Stars

THE CRAYONED STARS of my childhood in Helsinki, Finland, where my life began in 1946, have five points. With my bright yellow crayon, I'd press down on the somberly pitch-black sky so hard that the points of the stars practically bore holes through my coloring papers. *Five points, always must be five.* For this little Protestant girl, that's the way it is.

Till one day, crayons and paper before me at my two-seater wooden desk at school, I overlap two wobbly triangles and now my bright and shiny star has six points.

That's not the way a Northern star looks like, my first-grade teacher says with a scowl.

The heat from the silent shame of doing something wrong slowly creeps up the sides of my face. I'll never draw another star in class again. Only in our cramped four-story walk-up, where my sister and I share a tiny bedroom, will these sparkling symbols of something good continue to illuminate my vision of a happy life to come, just like in picture books and fairytales.

Many years later, settled as a young mother in the tropical metropolis of Miami, I marvel at the lavishness of teachers so freely handing out gilded stars to my own children. And I contemplate an earlier life that had shown me the true radiance of these celestial bodies, those I crayoned and those I watched in the Nordic sky.

How strange, then, that this new home of mine, in the Tropics no less, is where I'll be learning the truth about the King of Denmark and *his* star, the one that never was.

Mention "Denmark" and "Jews" in the same sentence to almost anyone of a certain age, and you'll get the story about how, during WWII, the Danish king wore the Yellow Star in solidarity with the Jews. The mythical proportion of the royal heroism is only matched by stories from Sweden, the supposedly neutral country said to have reached out with open arms to all Jewish refugees from Denmark.

But mention "Scandinavia" and the war years, and the response changes. Some people will blabber on about Switzerland while others speak vaguely about Sweden (… Swedish, Swiss; all the same, they sometimes say), but if you mention Norway and Finland in the same breath as Sweden or Denmark the reaction is usually one of befuddlement. Metaphorically scratching their heads, people then wonder why I'd include Norway. And *Finland*? It was, after all, the King of *Denmark* who…. Or was it?

At my middle school in post-war Helsinki, there'd been an occasional hint at the dark side of humanity having spread to Scandinavia during WWII, but with youthful selfishness I'd shrugged off any mention of Jews dying in camps as something irrelevant to me. The Nazis hadn't occupied my country, "just" Norway, our Western once-removed neighbor, and Denmark, the continental off-shoot across from the Nordic peninsula. And then there was Sweden, our immediate neighbor to the West, whose language we spoke at home and at school, making us part of a minority group of resident citizens of Finland.

Although I can't pinpoint the exact time when I became fascinated by the wartime actors in Scandinavia; for sure the slow process began in the '70s with Jewish-American friends in Miami asking about Denmark. When they learned I wasn't at all Danish but a *Swedish*-speaking Finn, born and raised in Helsinki, that seemed intriguing in South Florida where being an immigrant mostly meant being Hispanic. And since I straddled more than one Nordic country (Finland and Sweden), Jewish friends began looking at me as a direct line to information about what happened to their Scandinavian *landsmen* while the Holocaust was unfolding on the continent. As protection from my personal ignorance, and to please my questioners, I went looking for the historical facts on Denmark – only Denmark – but since this was prior to on-line information, I had to depend on the local library.

And then I remembered our Nordic Christmases with the Jewish themed books.

The year was 1960, when Santa Claus arrived on a bleak Saturday night. With him, Leon Uris was introduced to our home in Helsinki. Not in a physical shape, of course, but through his words.

Our family tradition called for at least one book for each of us three children, neatly buried in a heap of wrapped presents under the tree and to be opened that first evening of Christmas. Since December 25 and 26 were official state holidays with all commerce prohibited by law, the long-awaited gift of new reading material was entertainment during the long stretch of typical Christmas drudgery. My parents also abided by a strict social custom that called for staying at home on the 25th, a habit I continued with my own children without ever questioning the purpose of what now seems silly and without any foundation in reason. So deeply ingrained was this tradition then, that anyone making the mistake of dropping by for a visit on that day was promptly labeled a Christmas Swine.

It was also a family rule that my father chose the book-gifts. This he did either from the latest review in the Swedish-language newspaper or from what he discovered during his regular rounds to what was then the largest bookstore in Scandinavia, *Akademen*, smack in the middle of Helsinki.

3

And, so it came to be in 1960 that *Exodus* ended up under our tree, with my name on the package as well as inscribed by my father in the book itself.

From the fly page I saw the Swedish title was the same as the original English. A strange name that vividly brought to mind a memory of my middle school with its obligatory religious classes, where we took turns reading out loud from the Bible. In this particular recollection of my youth, someone had just finished stumbling his way through what we called the Second Book of Moses in the Old Testament. The "bad boys" in my class were fidgeting while I had my hands neatly folded on my desk. As the teacher droned on about how the Israelites were delivered from slavery, the monotony of his voice kept me from keeping up with the story line. I don't think I understood the significance of the Jewish exodus from Egypt until many decades later when, in Miami, I was invited to my first Passover.

Now, on Christmas Eve 1960, I could only hope the biblical overtone of that year's reading gift, *Exodus*, didn't mean more religious lessons. But so strong was my will not to disappoint my father that the very next day I began the book.

Soon I found I couldn't put it down. My empathy for those brave Jews who were interned in a Cypriote camp hoping to make it to Palestine knew no bounds. Somehow, I identified with their wish to leave home for another place they could call home. When I came to the passage about King Christian X of Denmark – imagine that, a Scandinavian! – my heart raced with pride. Here was one of "us" as a moral guide. And a royal person, at that.

I also read about the German occupiers decreeing all Danish Jews had to wear the Star of David, that infamous Yellow Star marking them as Jews, and how the king was the first one to put it on his sleeve. Presumably because the 1960 Otto Preminger movie *Exodus* (based on Uris's book) repeats the story about the king and the star, this myth then went on to live a long life of its own. Later, I'll discuss the truth behind that common legend.

Even with the maturity that comes with age and its distance to the past, it's hard for me to understand the constant guilt and fear I lived with till the day I moved away from home. My father's praise for my high grades was no substitute for mother's suspicion that I was going to misbehave in one way or the other. I was afraid of making friends, even on the university level, as I imagined them ridiculing me behind my back for not being part of their – really, *any* – group. One time, a friend gleefully said she'd overheard some law school classmates saying I'd never get married because I was "too independent." Whatever the meaning of that judgment of me as a person, the pain made me retreat further into myself.

It was also a mix of guilt over not being grateful, and the fear of being judged that stopped me from telling my father at Christmas 1966 that the books I really wished for that year were about Hollywood glamor, specifically something about a suave and elegant leading man named Clark Gable (who'd passed away that year). If that wasn't genteel enough under the tree, I hoped my father would pick from the prominent displays in the bookstores one or two of the glossy publications on the Swedish princesses and the little crown prince.

Instead, that Christmas Eve, I had to feign gratitude for his choice of Muriel Spark's *Mandelbaumporten*, the freshly translated edition of *The Mandelbaum Gate*. Not that it was the Swedish title that bothered me; after all, I never received anything written in the Finnish language, although sometimes my father would bring home works in German or English. Instead, I was taken back by the inside flaps of this book with the German-sounding name of a gate. Didn't my father know I didn't want a thriller, particularly one set in Israel during the times of the Eichmann trial in Jerusalem? Since his capture in Argentina in 1960, followed by his conviction a year later, journalists from all over Scandinavia had long been reporting the grisly facts presented as evidence of the Holocaust, but I knew I didn't have the courage to read more about that evil man. And yet, I found myself devouring *Mandelbaumporten*; probably from lack of other activities during the two quiet Christmas days when at least the world I knew had shut down.

Since the age of seven when I pictured myself a "world-famous writer," I remained an avid reader with my own library card, who'd scribbled those words on a homemade book cover. But now, decades after that childish yearning for fame, even the idea of putting on paper stories and facts about what happened to the Jews in Scandinavia during WWII ground to a halt when I contemplated the inevitable questions about me. Since I started giving presentations on the subject, I already knew there was no Q&A segment without someone being curious about me as a person. *Was I Jewish? Where did I come from? Why my interest in Scandinavian Jewry?*

At first I thought these questions had something to do with a recent abundance of media interest in the Nordic psyche, as it related to *hygge* (the simple life) and the way it was practiced as individual modesty in all areas of life. So deep-rooted was my unwillingness to share personal details that I went to great length to steer any questions about me, the lecturer, as a person, into the neutral territory of Scandinavian geography and history. With luck, my listeners responded the way I'd hoped.

They asked about Quisling, the infamous Norwegian prime minister, whose name is forever inscribed in the Oxford English dictionary as a synonym for traitor. They wondered what happened to Felix Kersten, Himmler's personal massage therapist from Finland looking almost physically attached to the evil Nazi leader on the pictures I showed. They wanted more about Rabbi Melchior in Copenhagen who, on the eve of the round-up, told his congregation to go into hiding. They even shared their own takes on the Swedes, some incredibly brave and some indifferent, even as these views related to the rescue efforts by Raoul Wallenberg, and Count Bernadotte with the White Buses. So, it seemed my plan to avoid talking about me worked.

Till, one day, I was interrupted by a tall burly man, who'd claimed a front-row seat by his early arrival. "Why don't you write a book about all this?" he wanted to know.

"No time," I said dismissively.

But the thought lingered, spurred as it was by more speeches and continuous prodding by sundry people. And as often happens in life, serendipity intervened. It came in the form of an elderly woman at my talk at the School of International & Public Affairs of Florida International University. I'd just finished when she grabbed my arm. Eyes brimming with purpose and with an air of total self-confidence, she looked like she might have been a distinguished professor in her past.

"You really need to write a book," she said, nodding her head between each word as for extra emphasis. "And you must tell us about yourself, too."

Surprising both of us, I said, "I'm in the process right now."

This wasn't hyperbole. As is often the case when I lecture, my mind goes to related things and while I'd been responding to questions at this particular event, I was already making mental notes for a book outline. For sure, I was "in the process."

Above all, I knew then that if I wanted to connect with my audiences, I had to bridge the gap between the personal and the universal. This meant somehow – I didn't know how – I had to deal with my deep-seated Scandinavian aversion to insert myself into any topic (*mustn't draw attention to self*).

A snail-paced organic evolution followed, till it was this book. By then, a variety of groups had long invited me to talk about the subject, which I initially framed as "during the Holocaust Years." Even though that was exactly the period I'd been asked to talk about (defined in the literature as 1941-45), some hosts asked me not to include the H-reference in the subject line, and since the events in Scandinavia began a year earlier with the occupation of Denmark and Norway, my switch to "the war years" made sense. Also, non-native speakers of English who don't recognize linguistic nuances had already said they misunderstood the initial subject to mean Scandinavia had its own Holocaust, so the choice was in essence made for me.

But then came the cynics. "All that needs to be said about historical figures has already been shared and dissected. Take Himmler, for instance... ."

Another skeptic said, "You'll be translating other people's work, and you probably need permission for that."

I countered with the obvious: I wasn't going to serve translated facts as a dry dish of this-is-what-happened. I'd already read memoirs by such wartime figures as Count Bernadotte and Felix Kersten, each made easy for me by their use of the language we had in common (Swedish), and I knew their anecdotes, not normally found in other books, would add interest to the historical events. They also prompted me to dig deep into my own life to find my emerging Jewish awareness.

California Here I Come

If I were to describe my journey from Helsinki to Miami, I'd simply have to include California even though I never lived there. That's because Santa Monica did something to the soul of my youth by creating an inexplicable longing that would hound me for the rest of my years in Finland.

It all begins with the gym at my middle school in Helsinki when I'm not yet a teen. The multi-purpose hall is crammed with a couple of hundred fellow students, all sitting in neat and orderly rows on long wooden benches dragged out for the purpose of giving us a view of the large white screen in the front. The sameness of our daily routine has been broken by a visitor from America. He's in Helsinki as a Fulbright scholar, and as such he goes to different schools to show a movie and talk about his country. Problem is my class is still two years away from learning English, so all we can do now is gawk at the American.

When he flashes a big grin at us, I marvel at his perfectly straight and gleamingly white teeth. He seems so kind I want to reach out to touch his hand, but I know I could be disciplined for unacceptable behavior like that, either by a teacher or, if I share this at home, by mother. Even though my classmates sit frozen from the anticipation, our homeroom teacher, a stern woman with a stiffly rolled bun on her head, motions to us to be silent. The principal then tells us in Swedish, for ours is a Swedish-speaking school, that we should all be excited over this very special treat of having a teacher come all the way from America – yes, *America*! – to show us a movie about young people in his home state. He's from Santa Monica, which is high above the Pacific Ocean in California, which is in America.

Even though I no longer remember the exact time of the year this was, I know our visitor arrived on one of those bleak and overcast days in Helsinki that later inspire me to journal about the long stretch of days when the sun doesn't peek out at all ("today is the 45th day without any sun"). As I'm about to find out, the only thing that'll cut through my melancholy life are the rays of the Santa Monica sun, which serves as a backdrop to all these beautiful boys and girls who seem to frolic from classroom to beach with a perpetual expression of thrill and happiness. And again those white teeth, so perfectly straight and shiny! I also marvel at the way the girls dress – whoever saw such playful shoes and bouncy skirts like that! – and I envy the ease with which they seem to talk with the boys and each other, even their teacher. The palm trees are swaying, and everybody is so very, very joyful.

The movie never leaves me, not even now more than 60 years later. Throughout my life in Helsinki, the memory of that day, later repeated by other American visitors, continues to feed an inexplicable longing in me. When the California sun cuts right through to my soul I feel the ache of wanting to fit in with that group of pretty and popular students.

But I still have to face the non-dreamy world in front of me. Life in war-damaged Helsinki with my parents and older brother and sister is doing its best to mold me into the kind of girl mother envisions.

The simplest way to generally describe Helsinki in the 1950s – the whole country of Finland, for that matter – is to say it was a homogeneous society, not exactly overrun by immigrants. The difficult Finnish language also added to a sense of national isolation, although the other official language – Swedish – was (still is) easier to master for anyone with a Germanic background, such as Yiddish-speakers.

So, what's with the Swedish? Americans will ask me. This is Finland, after all.

The short answer is that for almost 700 years, the country was ruled by Sweden so, in a sense, Swedish-speaking Finns are a remnant of that period, which ended in 1809 when Finland became a province (a "Grand Duchy") of Russia. That era lasted till 1917 when the country finally became independent, and the brand-new constitution guaranteed equal status to both languages (Finnish and Swedish).

In a practical sense, this means Finns with Swedish as their native tongue (this includes my whole family) are entitled to use their mother language at such places as health and day care centers, and all kinds of cultural institutions (such as the historical Swedish Theatre in Helsinki, from 1827). They also have their own schools, political party, and Swedish-speaking representatives in state and local governments. They may even fulfill their military service in a Swedish-language detachment, although these conscripts must learn commands in Finnish to avoid any confusion on the battlefield.

My only brother, five years older than I, chose to do his military service in a Finnish-speaking unit specifically to improve on the language he'd picked up in the streets and in the more formal setting of his Swedish-only school. For the rest of his life he's grateful to the armed forces for having perfected his Finnish.

Because we only speak Swedish at home and in the schools I attend, I develop an early sense of being separate from the larger society. My own Finnish is so bad that when, as mother's little helper, I'm sent to the store to buy the necessary tokens for our gas stove she makes me practice several times before I go. In a trembling voice I then say to the dour sales lady, "Haluaisin kolme polettia (I'd like three tokens)," in such a stilted way that it's a dead give-away I'm not a native Finnish-speaker. As a teen, when I beg my mother to let me do summer work on a Finnish-only farm – a common way to learn the language at that time – she cryptically says, it isn't "suitable." Our family must remain separate, above the lowbrow populace.

My parents spend an inordinate time instilling in their three children, more in the two girls than in the oldest, who's my brother, a sense of not being just anybody. By first grade I'm already aware of the differences between "them" (Finnish-speaking Finns) and us Swedish-speakers. The clear implication is that we Swedish-speaking Finns, although citizens of Finland by birth, are of a higher social standing than "regular Finns," and socializing with them isn't for us. We can only have "friends" – the quotation marks are appropriate since close bonds are out of the question – who come from what mother deems an acceptable pedigree.

When I try to explain the reasons for all this to my American friends, they are mostly puzzled.

"But, your parents must have been born in Sweden," they insist.

"No, no," I say. "We're Finns, but we spoke only Swedish at home and in my schools. Used to be, in my childhood, 10% of the population did that, but today the number is down to 5%. Either way, I'm still part of a linguistic minority."

I must have been around eight when a little boy (I've never forgotten his name, Erkki, which is Finnish for Erik) came up to me as I was bouncing a ball on the sidewalk by our apartment building. I'd only seen him at a distance, so I was horrified when he ran towards me and hissed, "Why don't you speak Finnish. This is Finland!" Then he kicked me in the shin with the metal-covered tip of his boot.

Many decades later, into the new century, I'll reflect on that kind of hatred and think how far we've come with spreading buzzwords like anti-bullying and international understanding. Or so I think. Till one day when I run across an interview with the president of the local Chabad (a Jewish Hasidic establishment) in one of the dailies in Helsinki. When he said it was easier to be a Jew than a Swede in the Finnish society, I despair. Not for the Jews but for a linguistic group still suffering from historical bias.

From an early age, my sister and I deal with this sense that we're different by pretending we're of royal birth. We invent "husbands" – hers is Phillip and mine Charles – and while they travel the world, we pretend we're in charge of the regal household at home. Then we fight over being the first to get our hands on

Svensk Damtidning, the ladies' weekly from Sweden, so we can spend hours dissecting every word, every tone struck by staffers assigned to do little else but follow the beat of all the royals.

Our parents add to this self-deception by constantly talking about how our family – we Finn-Swedes, never just "Swedes" – must live by the high standard of our class. Like the King of Sweden has his motto of "duty above all" our family must have one, too. Ours becomes "measured dignity" under all circumstances.

In our later teens, the pretense that we descend from aristocracy becomes the veneer that we carefully cultivate in how we present ourselves to the outside world. "You acted so royal," we compliment each other after a situation where the normal reaction should be anger or hurt, such as when being mercilessly teased – even bullied – by classmates for not being part of any groups. We're different because we don't smoke or swear, or talk about boys, and our speech is always grammatical. Even the way we dress isn't like the teenage fashion of the day.

We live directly across the street from the school where my father teaches religious history to students who hate the subject but know there's no other choice. The curriculum is set by rigid bureaucrats in the Ministry of Education and when it comes to "the government" we know there's strict conformity.

The janitor of our building is a known communist – at least that's what my parents whisper – and he wants to please his comrades by making us all scrimp on heat and water so Finland's heavy war debt to the Soviets is paid off on schedule. On the few days he fires up the big boilers in the basement we celebrate by taking a hot bath, but we can never make plans. Sometimes it's on a Thursday and a Friday, at other times maybe on a Saturday and a Monday; even just one day. Because of his power over the hot water, I'm too afraid to look up when passing him in the barely lighted stairway, which I climb as fast as I can before the dim bulbs go completely dark again.

To the west of our building is a military garrison – parts of it still in ruins from Soviet bombers – which provides an exciting diversion from my life that's increasingly filling with inexplicable dread and a sense of alienation from the community. Strangely, the sight of the military band on its daily march to and from the changing of the guards at the nearby presidential palace uplifts me with the strong rhythm of the percussive instruments banging out a steady oompah-pah.

Just a few feet east of our apartment building is the German Lutheran Church, built in 1864 and, for its unique Gothic style, used as a popular wedding venue for the Swedish-speaking population. Three long blocks away, in the opposite direction, is what we call "play school," although it's really a privately owned Swedish-language kindergarten, where I'm allowed to walk by myself when I turn six. Real schooling doesn't start until I'm seven.

Sometimes during the early years of my childhood, long before the Santa Monica sun comes into my horizon, it becomes clear that mother could have been a star, probably an opera singer or concert pianist because of her inherited musical talent. One of her forefathers wrote the lyrics to one of the most cherished folk music tunes (*Slumrande toner*) among the Swedish-speaking population in Finland. Never mind, he's been dead since 1927; he can still be dragged out as proof of mother being somebody if only…., the litany of her "if-only"s depends on her unpredictable mood on any given day.

Our father, on the other hand, comes from admittedly modest tillers in the country but went on to become an academic. Unfortunately for him, his field is religious history (with a minor in philosophy and psychology), a very sore spot with his mother-in-law, my Momma, who has no use for religiosity of any kind and Lutheran piety in particular. When she visits us in the summers, father quietly disappears to the little shed next to our cottage where he spends hours carving pieces of wood into little human figures and long-legged birds, all with primitive hand tools from his youth. When I'm a teenager and brave enough to ask him about Momma being so mean to him, he'll only quote the Bible passage about turning the other cheek.

Before we're royalty, my sister and I are ruled by our mother alone. So, when she says it's time for us to make the biennial visit to *Nylandsgatan* (the

Swedish name is right under the Finnish *Uudenmaankatu* on the street signs), less than a kilometer from where we live, we have no choice but to follow her lead. With a nod at Finland's historical ties to the Czarist Empire, we generically refer to mother's chosen shop as a *lafka* in the Russian vernacular, instead of the Swedish *butik*. The Finnish word *kauppa* never crosses our lips.

As she weaves her way through the tightly packed stacks of clothing, the search is on for just the right pair of long winter pants. But first she must locate the owner, whom she usually finds in a corner bent over a stack of sales receipts under the dim light hanging overhead. Then she straightens her round frame in the heavy black wool overcoat with the frayed edges. In the uptight but immaculately polite voice she uses when dealing with people she considers beneath her in social standing, she makes it distinctly clear she's there for one thing only and that's the sturdiest and longest-lasting "ski"-pants for her two girls. This word sounds more sophisticated than the alternative Swedish "long" pants, as if we were going to wear them at a ski resort on the continent, something I had only vaguely heard about.

Already as a five-year old I can feel my cheeks flush as I slip into a pair pulled from a pile of possibilities. In front of the owner I have to bend over with my hands down to the floor while mother gropes for room to grow. The heavy-duty, felt-like material, usually in black or midnight blue with elastic binding at the bottom of the legs, makes me itch.

But the thing I hate the most is still to come.

I make goot deal, the owner says.

His accent is heavy, a dead give-away of his Eastern-European roots, although there's no telling if he's a recent immigrant to Finland.

Ve-e-ry goot buy for you, he goes on.

He says all this in Swedish and, much to mother's already creeping annoyance, he repeats himself with the "best price."

This is when mother cocks an eyebrow and purses her lips in that unmistakable expression I've already learned is a sign of her discomfort and, therefore, also mine. At this early age, I know there's no such thing as

15

bargaining in Finland (although it'd be years before I understand about strict government price controls, which, for years to come, permit sales only at limited times of the year), so why is this man talking about "best price" and "good deal?" I resent him for making my mother uncomfortable.

Although she remains silent, it's obvious she's insulted. Whatever the amount, she hands him the cash without a word.

On the way home, mother mutters about Jews and their businesses. She must have forgotten her own gentile family were owners of a fur tannery and several shoe stores (though, mostly lost to alcoholism), the frequent domain of the Jewish population in Finland. She's not about to burden her little girls with that kind of talk now. Much too undignified.

My sister and I only listen when mother sighs, "Aah, the Jews and their *lafkas* …" We know better than to ask questions. Those half sentences just hang in the air of my memory bank.

As I get older I think it wasn't that she disliked the lafka-owner for being Jewish; after all, he did speak Swedish. It was just that he was in obvious breach of the prevailing social norms by offering to bargain; – a definite insult to mother's social standing, as if she didn't have the means to pay the full price.

The Jews sure are from a different world.

And in Finland they are. The original population came from the young boys the Czar conscripted for his army, sometimes grabbing thirteen-year olds off the streets in Russia. The cantonist system required them to serve for at least twenty-five years but afterwards they were allowed to remain in Finland, still an autonomous part of Russia. These former conscripts are then the beginning of the Jewish community in our country, where Helsinki remains home for the largest Jewish congregation with 1,500 members.

Only allowed to engage in certain kinds of business, the first Jewish settlers primarily traded in old clothing in stalls – *lafkas* – on the Russian market square in Helsinki. It was not unusual for them to become fluent in Swedish, like mother's *lafka*-owner, because they quickly found that Yiddish shared linguistic roots with Swedish and, therefore, making it easier for them to make themselves understood in this new language as opposed to the more complicated Finnish. Later Jewish immigrants, even refugees from Nazi Germany, also soon discovered the abundance of Swedish-language schools, newspapers, and government officials, all of which made commerce and assimilation easier.

By 1952 Finland's debt to the Soviet Union is paid off and three years later the government-mandated price controls are gone. The Jewish owner of the *lafka* where mother continues to buy ski pants for her girls still gives her every opportunity to "make deal" but throughout her life she'll distance herself from overtly *bargaining* because in her opinion it's demeaning for someone of her high-class background.

In 1956 when I'm ten, the uprising in Hungary increases public fear, and therefore the tension in our family, that the Soviets are just waiting to invade Finland. My parents talk about the possibility of a communist revolution or, worse, an outright war against our monstrous neighbor to the East. Instead, there's a 19-days long general strike throughout the country, brought on by the demands for a wage increase by the labor unions. As services and transportation come to a total stand-still, mother manages to get herself and me tickets on a train to a family-style lodge outside Helsinki, where the brutal March winds drive us to stuffing newspapers in the window frames so we can preserve some heat in the small cot-type beds, which are probable remnants from the war.

It's also around this time that I'm allowed to have a best friend.

She comes from a "fine" family, which means she has a last name that meets with mother's approval. The fact that her father is a top executive with one of the largest industries in Finland doesn't hurt either. They live in a large apartment on the top floor of the building next to us, where her family sips water with dinner, not prosaic whole milk like us. Her school – Swedish-language, of course – is a tram's trip away while mine is almost around the corner. Her classmates are adventuresome and high-spirited while mine are like me, scared conformists.

"I have a Jewish boy in my class," she tells me one day in a voice that says this is something extraordinarily quaint and glamorous. I'm full of marvel and envy and can't wait to meet him. When I do, my disappointment knows no bounds. He looks like us, plays like us, and even speaks Swedish like us.

When he walks her home on a day when she's not allowed to go out to play, they'll talk with each other through the heavy wooden door. One day, when I'm next to her in the foyer of her apartment, she presses her mouth to the brass mail-slot and shouts,

"A Jew, a Jew, with bended nose;

curly curls and crooked toes."

I'm in awe over her ability to rhyme. She's so grown-up. She even knows how babies are made.

I don't tell her I have no idea what a Jew is.

The Clown Prince And Me

Summers at our little cottage by the seashore are three long months of anxious tedium. While my brother is allowed to hang out with the sons of the local farmer, the message is clearly communicated by mother that we girls are not to play with local children. They are country and we're big city. Even though I have a second-hand bike, I'm mostly confined to home, where I quickly learn anything considered frivolous behavior will be punished with stony silence by mother. The water is too cold for swimming, and I won't help out with our little garden again since my parents laughed so heartily when I plucked a lily instead of a leek for dinner. I'm not even allowed to take the bus into the closest town, *Jakobstad*, to check out books from the library. All I can do is pretend, and hope; for *what*, I'm not certain.

Twice-a-summer visits by Momma provide a welcome release from the doldrums. Not only is she the one who teaches me how to play cards, but her risqué jokes and the occasional obscenity when she can't light her ever-present cigarette, emboldens me to stick a toe into mother's icy disapproval that's certain to ensue if I break the familial code of dignified behavior.

One summer evening when we once again hover next to our small transistor radio for a music program from Sweden, Momma tells me about Victor Borge. In lively terms that involve large sweeps with her cigarette, she describes how he'd fall off his piano bench in the middle of a piece. Lacking any actual re-enactment (we have neither piano nor bench) I can only imagine someone so brazenly funny that he'd do something like that in public. I laugh till I cry.

And to think he's "one of us," as she says.

Naturally, mother finds even talk of antics totally unacceptable and she also corrects her own mother that Victor is from *Denmark* – not Finland – and he's Jewish, not Protestant. I never could decide what it means to be "one of us" although Momma also said she read how he'd taken a passenger ship to America. Since the only port remaining open in Scandinavia happened to be on the Finnish side of the Nordic peninsula, maybe that's what made it seem to her that if it weren't for us, Victor would've perished in the Holocaust nightmare.

Even with my own vivid imagination, fed by Momma's descriptive tales about our fellow Scandinavian, I couldn't have envisioned the scene that was to take place in the late 1980s on a beautiful May evening outside the ballroom of a luxury hotel in Manhattan. I'd flown up there with my dance partner from Miami, a retired manual laborer for an airline and a dependable escort with impeccable manners. The women in our dance group fought over him because of his great skills on the dance floor; it was quite obvious that some of them wanted him all to themselves. For me, he held no romantic interest and the best thing about him was that he loved Borge, the Clown Prince of Denmark, as much as I did.

My evolving sense of freedom in America had long inspired me to express myself artistically in all kinds of ways, including tailoring and pattern-making techniques, all in my quest to create my own clothing that seemed to get the attention I must have craved for my new self. With the latest *haute couture* of the Nordic royals prominently featured in my beloved *Svensk Damtidning*, passed on locally between Swedish friends, I never lacked for inspiration. For a dinner in honor of visiting King Olaf of Norway, I purchased inexpensive fabric in three different but complementary polka dot designs and, copying what I'd seen in the Swedish journal, fashioned evening pants, a tunic, a braided belt and a tie for the royal event. Evoking the interest of a Miami *Herald* reporter, my garb (by a "Finnish designer") was then immortalized in a picture appearing in the paper just a couple of days later.

Now, for the New York event with the Comedian of the Keyboard I decided to match my evening outfit with my sentiments of fun and adventure. For a month, I'd worked on the design of a below-the-knee-length dress – today I'd call it a *costume* – in the colors of all the Scandinavian flags (blue, white, red, yellow). It had a flowing, tiered skirt that flounced all around me when I moved, and I fashioned a cross-strap from shoulder to waist of actual table-size flags, done in such a way as to avoid any flapping in one of many snappy cha-chas.

From his perch on the baroque settee, Victor looked me up and down when I entered. We shook hands and I thought I heard him say with the usual twinkle of amusement in his eyes, "I see you like flags." It wasn't until my dance partner and I closed down the dance floor at 11 pm that I heard a waitress snicker to another, "Can you *believe* what she's wearing." Her tone could have been that of mother, definitely disapproving. If only she knew the long history Victor and I shared.

Some ten years later, when I'm giving presentations to a Miami audience eager to learn more about Denmark during WWII, I'll be telling listeners that the Great Dane had been performing in the Swedish capital, Stockholm, when he received a call from his wife in Copenhagen that German planes were dropping thousands of pamphlets all over the capital. The infamous date was April 9, 1940, the day of Hitler's invasion of both Denmark and Norway. Short of suspecting circumstances for European Jews were about to worsen, nobody was quite certain about the future of either country.

On a whim, Victor decided to head to the US Consulate in Stockholm, where he was warmly received by a consul, already a fan of his. With an American visa in hand he was then able to reach the Finnish port of *Petsamo* by the Arctic Sea, a strategically vital site for the Soviets who later claimed it for themselves in the armistice with Finland. The story goes that he literally jumped onto the gangplank of the last American vessel to leave Europe; the name of the ship was either the American *Legion* or *Legend*, depending on the source one believes. When it finally pulled into the New York Harbor on August 28, 1940, the NYT was waiting for an interview with the master of the ship, not some unknown Danish piano player who didn't speak a word of English. While Victor didn't complain over having arrived with only $20.00 in his pocket, the captain is on record with his rage over not having been warned about the minefields on the ocean he'd just crossed. But in the end, the ship and passengers were safe and that was the only thing that really mattered.

Although the future Clown Prince of Denmark was safely in America, as an only child he didn't forget about his responsibility toward an ailing mother left behind in Copenhagen. Once during the five years of Nazi occupation, and disguised as a sailor, he managed to return to his home country to visit her. Wearing a protective mask to her hospital room he told his dying mother a lie he'd remember for the rest of his life. Børge Rosenbaum, her son who was now Victor Borge, had already been given a large Hollywood contract! As he says in recorded interviews, fortunately she didn't ask how that was possible since he still didn't speak a word of English.

I may also tell my listeners that the Great Dane lived a long happy life in his beloved new homeland of America while never forgetting his country of birth. Before he died at the age of 91, he made sure half of his ashes was to be interred in the Jewish cemetery in Copenhagen. Hence, part of Victor Borge returned to his beginnings in a country where the roots of the Jews ran deep, at least to the 17th century when the king had invited them (first the *Sephardi*, then the *Ashkenazim*) to help modernize Denmark. Preparing for my presentations I also learned that the Danish Jews were given full and equal protection in 1814, and during that century they prospered as pioneers in both business and politics. Along the way they became an intrinsic part of Danish society.

Stars, Catholics and Jews

In the summer of 1952, a unique kind of stars descends on Helsinki. These are the top athletes from around the world coming for the summer Olympics in a country that many of them only know as "brave little Finland" from the international press reports on how it stood up to the Soviet giant during the war. *This should already have been us in 1940,* some Finns say to each other while overlooking the fact that no country in the world could have hosted the games in the middle of what was then WWII. Because of the Japanese alliance with Nazi Germany, Tokyo, the first choice for that year, was obviously out of the question, and the runner-up, Helsinki, couldn't do anything else but try to stay alive after the Soviet attack of Finland three months after the world was at war.

Maybe in an effort to use sports to bring some sanity to everyone, between the cancelled games of 1940 and Finland hosting them in 1952, nations had somehow managed to pull themselves together so that London (even with visible remnants from the Nazi *Blitzkrieg*) had welcomed the first post-war Olympics in 1948. Still banned for having started WWII, Japan and Germany weren't then allowed to send teams to the British capital but now, at the 1952 summer games in Helsinki, they're very much present, along with star athletes from first-ever participating countries like the Soviet Union and Israel. Although my sister and I are too young to understand the meaning of what some reports called the *Jewish teams*, there's a real new sense of global awareness in our family.

My father, a war veteran himself, likes to talk about Finnish stamina (*"sisu"*) both in defending the country and in the sports arena. He makes sure my sister and I make the long trek to the stadium, already inaugurated in 1938, where there's a huge bronze statue of a man he wants us to see. Seemingly posed for another victory in these 1952 summer games, Paavo Nurmi, the "Flying Finn," had already brought home a gold medal from the Antwerp (Belgium) games in 1920, but now during the Helsinki games he isn't allowed to compete. Instead, the picture and movie-clips of him lighting the torch goes out around the world as a beacon for his courageous homeland, which, miraculously, had survived two recent wars against the Soviets without any assistance by most of the Olympic countries now in Helsinki.

Even with the games over, the endless hikes with my father through the city and its immediate environs continue. When our meanderings take us through the diplomatic section of Helsinki, he averts his eyes from the massive Soviet Embassy, the grey granite and covered windows making it appear both lackluster and scary. If he sees me steal a forbidden peek at it, he curses under his breath and yanks my arm to indicate that we must walk faster. At a good fifteen-minutes distance from the diplomatic enclaves, his stance visibly softens when he stops in front of a fenced-in building of which I only remember an unusual cupola. In a soft voice that's in stark contrast to our Soviet encounters, he says, "This is where the Jews go to pray." He also says we can't step inside because, unlike the churches that are always open to the public, the synagogue – the only one in Helsinki – is locked. It isn't until much later in my teens, for some long-forgotten reason, that I finally am able to enter this mysterious place of worship. My only memory of the inside of the building is a picture of Marshall Mannerheim next to leaders of the congregation, one of whom is a Mr. Kagan, whose name I already associate with the eponymous antiques store on the prestigious *Boulevard*. I'll be talking more about him in another chapter.

Maybe because I spend more time with my father than my sister and brother do, and maybe because I physically resemble him, I form an early impression of being his favorite child. This makes it easy for me to share things I can't verbalize with any other person, such as my anguish-filled worries about my future; since Santa Monica, this has come to mean getting away to some other place than Finland. He offers no direct advice on my fuzzy dreams, and will only say, "Walking helps you think." Later in life I understand how listening was his gift to me.

As I said, my budding international awareness began with Finland hosting the Olympics. American visitors to our school continued to inspire me to seek out Hollywood movies with some sort of foreign angle like Audrey Hepburn provided in *The Nun's Story* (naturally sub-titled in both languages of Finland). After watching it twice, I announced to my father that I wanted to be a nun who goes to Africa to care for the sick population. Not that I had any knowledge of Catholicism and its institutions (at that time, the Finnish population was 98% Lutheran), but the few Catholics I'd read about seemed glamorous and glitzy. Jews were in the same category, different in a "good" way. Besides, the nature of the group of people didn't matter as long as they accepted me.

Again, my father listened in earnest to my babble. But this thing with being a nun visibly upset him. As far as he went, there was only one religion and that was Protestantism. Catholicism was nonsense. About Judaism he said, "Jesus was a Jew, you know" as if that explained anything.

In the sea of Finnish Protestantism of the '50s and '60s, Judaism barely made a ripple. If there was anything out of the ordinary about the "other religions," which we superficially studied at school, it was more my youthful attraction to unfamiliar customs that captivated me purely because they stood out, although not always in a good sense. For instance, our family would snicker at an unconventional ladies' hat and say, "that's a real *Methodist* bonnet," as if we even knew someone of that religious background. In 2016, when books on *hygge* were topping American bestseller lists, one writer discussed the uniformity of the Nordic society and how someone (in this case, a Norwegian) would even be ridiculed for wearing a hat considered "different." Since he was mum on religious headgear, I didn't learn from him where on the tolerance scale Scandinavians stood with Jewish skull caps.

When it came to Judaism, I – for no discernible reason other than wanting to gain recognition of some kind – chose *Pesach* as the subject for an essay on holidays we had to write when I was twelve. Maybe because I called it "Jewish Easter" and I was the only one writing on a non-Lutheran topic, the grade for my otherwise flawless piece was tarnished by the tiny minus that followed. This left me feeling victimized for years afterwards as I regretted having been too different.

Although I wasn't then aware of the ancient, mysterious road-map for Scandinavian behavior (as some claim, since the time of the Vikings), the fact that there were strict principles deeply embedded in my DNA made me instinctively know it was always better to blend in, to conform to very set expectations. Satirically summarized in a novel from 1933 as the ten rules of *Jante's Law*, this doctrine is part of my genetic heritage, in constant conflict with my natural yearning to be treated as an individual. "Always think for yourself," my father had told me many times. "Crowd thinking can lead to the kind of mass hysteria that killed the Jews."

At the time he and I had these conversations, I knew nothing about the individualism advocated by the Danish philosopher, Kierkegaard, and indirectly by my father. Since then, popular writings often refer to "Nordic individualism," as if this is as a magic bullet for the pain caused by my genetic and societal heritage. Today, I believe it's simply an over-rated concept used to explain why Scandinavians have a different approach to life than, say, Americans. I only see the ongoing demand for strict conformity, still evident in the media and among friends and relatives. Words like tyranny of thought and intolerance of other opinions often come to my mind when I try to describe this common attitude.

I believe as we age, we'll ponder the past and contemplate the inevitable end, perhaps even finding an explanation for who we've become. In this process I may have an advantage over my two siblings, since I've been journaling since I was seven. More than seventy journals later – all of which have made it through inter-continental and interstate moves – I still do it. Some people believe diarists write for deep psychological reasons, such as loneliness or feelings of being on the outside of society, but others argue it's just an easy way of keeping track of one's life. I know why I do it: I wasn't permitted a voice when I was a child, so I turned inwards.

In my journals I also recorded my father's gift for finding the deeper meaning in life ("let go and let God"), wanting to emulate his belief that we shouldn't fight the natural ebb and flow of life. And when my teenage needs for guidance from a mother with her own internal struggles weren't met, I shared my pain with the diaries. Many years later, I see how this was also my way of trying to understand why my family had no compassion for her imaginary or real ailments as we mercilessly ignored or teased her. "Maybe all she wanted in her misery was to be loved by me," I noted then in a more forgiving mode.

Re-reading my journals from the '50s I see a girl with a growing ability to latch on to tiny pleasures while trying to balance the cultural and familial demands for seriousness and decorum. In one early entry I'm almost giddy over moments when we were allowed to "play games" and "laugh almost all the time." In the summer when our transistor radio provided more entertainment than we had during the rest of the year in the city, I copied in my notebook the words to a cheerful American pop-song, *Sugartime*. Without understanding the meaning of the words, for they were, after all, in English, I sang the tune while pretending I was an American girl in Santa Monica. For Grace Kelly's fairytale wedding (*Catholic*!) to Prince Rainier in April of 1956 my sister and I begged our parents for money to send her a congratulatory note. The royal response was a postcard-size picture of the happy couple, which I kept tucked away through all my moves in America till, 60 years later, I finally hand it to the local Consul of Monaco. "This is part of your history, not mine," I say.

When a new girl joined our fourth-grade class I was immediately attracted to her dark curls and big brown eyes, although her natural smile worried me. All of us already knew how to dutifully fix on our faces the non-smiling, tight-lipped, studious look that expected and rewarded by our teachers. So when she became a no-show in our compulsory religious class, the whispering started. Had she done something wrong? Was she sick? Could she be … *Catholic*? … *Jewish*? Exemptions were only given to non-Protestants, we all knew that.

Finally, word reached us. *She was a Jew.*

Now I was overwhelmed by envy. Why couldn't I be special like her?

In my Helsinki of the '60s, the palm trees of Santa Monica don't stop their siren-like calls to me, as I continue to create ongoing fantasies about leaving my lonely life behind. Only in moments of harsh reality do I remind myself I must have a plan. First, at eighteen I must finish the *Gymnasium* and, then, a degree will follow naturally from the University of Helsinki (or, *Helsingfors* as the venerable university is called in Swedish, founded in 1640 when Finland was still part of the Swedish Empire). I know I want to enter a discipline that helps me move away, but which one?

It's at this time that mother steps in with her idea for a project-of-*class* (not to be confused with the *class* projects that are such an integral part of American education). Hers is now a case of making sure one of her three pedigree children is launched on a path in life that she'll later tell me she wishes she'd had. In this case, it looks like I'm the Chosen One.

"How would you like to go abroad to take a course of some kind this summer? You'd meet a lot of fine people," she says.

I wait. Surely there must be a catch here. If she thinks it's my lofty idea to go to the continent, I know she'll invoke her favorite refrain which is, *Who do you think you are*? Neither one of us knows her tone is one that I'll later be laughing over as the voice of the stereotypical, impossible-to-please Jewish-American mother.

"As my graduation gift…?" I finally say.

"Yes, I thought you'd like that. You'd meet people from other countries and… who knows…"

"Maybe this is the summer for the Crown Prince of Sweden," I joke. "Or that British Lord." Underlying the levity is what I imagine about the continent swarming with potential boyfriends of the highest standards.

Now in a happy mood, she laughs along with me. "But you can't go alone, so start thinking of someone who can join you."

I already know the perfect companion, whom I had recently met at a school event. She's two years older than me – clearly spelling maturity in mother's mind – but the critical part is her family name showing she's of good old Swedish-Finnish aristocracy.

"I'll ask Anita," I say, still not believing the turn my life seems to be taking. Thanks to mother, no less.

But then, the catch.

Emotionally erratic, mother now returns to her role as a naysayer when she points out what both of us knew all along. If I'm away for the summer, she says, my blather about enrolling in medical school must come to an immediate end even though this is the last year someone may be automatically admitted based on high grades alone. Although I fulfill all academic requirements, I'll be missing the mandatory in-person registration. My current fantasy of becoming a physician traveling widely outside the boundaries of Finland quickly fades before my eyes.

When she says, "You wouldn't make a good doctor at any case because you don't have that caring personality like your sister," I accept any offering by her must come with a price.

Now at the age of eighteen, there's an instant re-play in my mind of oft-repeated scenes from my early years: my ever-dying mother wants us girls to sit by her bed-side to hold and stroke her hand. I can't have been more than 5 or 6 years old, but I still feel the repulsion as I dreaded the thought of having to touch her white limpid flesh. On some childish level I knew this was an act, in which my sister was the good girl and I was doomed to be anything but that.

"I'll go to law school instead," I now tell her. "I won't miss the deadline for *that* enrollment."

And that's how the future course of my life is set in a matter of seconds.

Geneva *Mittos*

In the spring of 1965, I spring into action to find the right summer program at the right place in the right country, somewhere on the continent. Geneva and Switzerland have a good ring to them. Plenty of royalty have gone through Swiss finishing schools, most excitingly the youngest daughter of the King of Denmark, Princess Anne-Marie. Just a year before, she'd married Constantine, the movie-star handsome King of Greece, setting in motion another one of my royal fantasies.

Fortunately, there's International Organizations, a summer course offered in Geneva. It seems to come with the right touch of class, and above all, mother likes it. When she goes to the little neighborhood shop – we call it a "milk store" because it sells only the daily necessities – she tells the familiar sales lady her youngest daughter will be spending the summer at the University of Geneva, studying international organizations. "Switzerland," she adds for extra effect, lest the clerk doesn't get the exclusiveness of this venue.

When Anita and I arrive in Geneva, the private quarters we had been promised aren't available. Would the dorm do for us Finns? Or were we perhaps Swedish because of our last names? The registrar says she recognizes the Germanic roots because she deals with students from all over the world. But her curiosity turns to a bored shrug when I echo mother's life-long teachings on how this member of a fine Swedish-Finnish family expects a certain standard of housing accommodations.

Finally, after whispered deliberations with someone on the phone, the clerk sends us on our way with a residency slip to the *Cité Universitaire*. To us Finns this is a high-rise although not like the New York City skyscrapers I've seen in movies. The place is bustling with students from around the world, gathering either in the kitchenettes on each floor, or in the social quarters downstairs. We're assigned separate rooms (*our obviously high social standing got each of us a direct view of the snow-capped Swiss Alps*) where we eagerly study the packed schedule of our upcoming lectures. The program also promises exciting field trips to the international organizations with headquarters in Geneva.

On the day of our scheduled appointment at the ILO (International Labor Organization), Anita comes down with an inexplicable chill. Should I stay at home to care for my friend or would she understand if I went on the excursion since she knows I have my eye on a cute American boy? Long forgotten is mother's label of the non-caregiver. This is solely about me and the promise of having fun away from home.

When one of the international students on our floor says, "Go. I'll check on your friend," I'm happily off for the day.

After a successful day (*He spoke with me*), I find Anita sitting up in bed with a bowl of chicken soup in her lap. Her dark-haired helper introduces herself as "Pouran from Iran."

And then Anita says something startling. "You know, Pouran comes from a very large Jewish family and her father, who's a doctor, is talking about leaving Iran. I was saying they should come to Finland."

At that, Pouran laughs as if the thought of living in my home country is something so outrageous as to make it funny. When she cleans up the soup bowl, I stammer something about how unusual it is for a fellow student to be helping out like this. With my tentative English I don't understand what I think she's saying in response, "It's part of our *mittos*." At any case, I must present myself as internationally sophisticated so I can't ask about the meaning of something I should probably know.

It'll take ten years and a move to America before I understand what "Pouran from Iran" had said.

Mitzvahs! The good deeds Jews perform as a way of life.

I return home from Geneva with an uneasy awareness of countries where Jews may no longer feel welcome, like Pouran in Iran, although I don't understand how the homeland of royalty like Queen Soraya (and her handsome shah) could be one of them. For years, my sister and I have eagerly observed her for fashion and style in our usual Swedish weekly. On the other hand, we've also long empathized with Empress Farah Diba, the forerunner of current Queen Soraya, for unceremoniously having been tossed out from Iran because she couldn't give the shah an heir. If a royal ruler really acted like that, maybe – just maybe – he should have the power to make his country safe for Pouran's father.

All this thinking about Jews not being safe makes me uncomfortable. And curious.

I want to talk, don't know exactly about what, with any law school classmate who might be Jewish, but "I know about your *mittos*," sounds too patronizing, and I'm not even sure I should bring something up that I don't know yet what it is. And, "Excuse me, but are you Jewish (or Swedish, or American, or German or any other ethnicity for that matter)?" isn't something Finns would say to anyone. In fact, the taciturnity of people in Finland is now a phenomenon widely observed and discussed by visitors from other countries.

It was around this time that a story spread around the university about a Fulbright professor from America, who was teaching an English conversation class. Someone read, or heard, about his bitter complaint to his Finnish colleagues that it was impossible to engage his students in even the briefest of oral practice. One day, out of frustration when he asked a question and got no answer from anyone, he allegedly pointed a finger at one of the students in the front row and said, "*Say something* or I'll shoot you."

"Shoot me," said the student, not knowing that this simple response captured the essence of the whole Finnish population in one brief stroke.

My return home from Geneva also comes with a new sense of independence that brings on mother's angry disapproval. She's not happy with me spending time socializing with fellow law students, both female and male, so she interrogates me about every detail about them (their family names, background, prior grades, future plans). And then there's that ever-present threat of her impending death, repeated with great regularity and evidenced by her growing depression and anxieties over being left alone in the apartment. When I complain to my father, he says in his usual laconic way, "Laugh it off," but sometimes he's practically verbose when he offers another set of favorite words of comfort, "By the time you're a bride you'll be fine."

Although the romantic image of being a bride in a white veil and with a pearly princess crown in the wedding style of the day usually uplifts me, now the thought of having to answer to some ordinary husband – horror of horrors, a Finnish-speaking man, maybe? – makes me queasy from the anxiety. Not to mention the requisite marital sex, of which I have no idea what it really entails and therefore feel nothing but fear. I don't even have a boyfriend and I'm still a live-at-home law student with one single goal and that's to graduate as fast as possible so I can launch myself onto an international career of some kind. Mother need not worry, I say quietly to myself when she rages about me being "secretive" about everything surrounding my daily routine.

In my second semester at law school, when I re-visit memories of Pouran and the soup scene, I have another Jews-and-their-food incident, this one involving a Mr. Kagan, the eponymous owner of a large antiques store on the prestigious *Boulevard* in Helsinki. Mother, who liked antique *objets d'art*, often spoke about him with reverence, as if he were a rare find himself. Although I'd been passing by his shop window for years, I don't meet him in person until a year later. And, as I said, that event centers around food.

The venue is a dinner meeting of the Lions Club, held at the exclusive Swedish Club. Here, we must understand that the concept of private clubs in general was quite unknown in Finland. The nobility had their House of Nobility, a relic from the centuries when we were a part of Sweden, but events at that "club" were generally limited to the titled members.

The Swedish Club, patterned on the British gentleman's club, was founded in 1880 (when Finland was still a Russian Grand Duchy) as a place for men; first to nurture their native Swedish tongue and later, to find ways to protect the language and culture during a time of *Finnomania* and tightened controls by Czar Alexander III (also infamous for enacting over 300 antisemitic regulations).

Membership in the Swedish Club was open to any male, after a vote, with the endorsement of two existing members. The unwritten rule was that men void of substance and achievement need not apply but like with many a segregated country club in the US there was little said openly about these shrewd reasons for denying membership to someone.

One time, when my father seemed unusually happy to have been invited to the club by a former student of his who had made it big in one of the industries, I asked him why he didn't become a member.

"What for? I don't need to stand out," he said.

For emphasis, he then added one of his cherished Bible quotes, "The first shall be the last and the last shall be the first."

The philosophy he shared by this statement, and which I'd learned to recognize as an integral part of Finnish culture and rules of behavior, was that one must never think one is better than anyone else. And what says that more than an exclusive membership? Still, he'd long and cheerfully accepted invitations for dinner at this elitist club. Now when I, his youngest daughter, am asked to appear before an illustrious group of men at this place, he simply can't contain his satisfaction.

The reason for the honor bestowed on me was that I'm the winner of a peace essay contest held by the Lions Club of *Helsingfors* (here, the Swedish name of Helsinki is appropriate because the language of the club was Swedish-only). When I receive the call about the prize, which was nothing but an ornate certificate, I'm invited to their dinner meeting where I'm going to read my essay aloud.

On Thursday night, February 10, 1966, at the appointed time – in my family we're so punctual we arrive early to walk around on a snowy sidewalk for minutes rather than ringing a door bell too early – I arrive to a disheartening sight: Waitresses in black uniforms with small white aprons are already scurrying about with the customary post-dinner coffee and cognac. Obviously, the Lions, all of them old men in my view, are at the end of their meals.

One of the members sees me standing by the coat check, self-conscious and unsure. He's unusually broad-shouldered and has what seems like a large head with more hair than any of my male relatives. He comes towards me with an outstretched hand.

In the customary way of Finland, he then introduces himself with his surname only. "Kagan," he says with a slight bow from the waist as we shake hands.

When he invites me to sit next to him, he asks if I'd like to have dinner. I can't understand why I'm put in a spot where I have to say out loud in front of all these men that, yes, I'd like some food. *Why wouldn't I? You're the ones who invited me! Couldn't you just bring me a plate with whatever you'd eaten?*

Like my mother wanting the *lafka*-owner to size her up as a member of the upper class who didn't need or want favors from anyone, I suddenly know I can't accept charity from these Lions. Although my stomach reminds me I'd skipped dinner at home, I regally decline.

"Thank you very much but I've already eaten," I lie.

"Sorry to hear that," says Mr. Kagan. "Maybe I can get you something to drink then? A beer? A cognac?"

Now, what do I do? I'm not used to alcohol of any kind, because mother doesn't permit it at home. *But wait, father always says a real lady can have a glass of cognac...*

And that's how I end up a bit tipsy next to Mr. Kagan.

At home, my excited parents want a play-by-play report. *Our youngest daughter's been a guest at the Swedish Club!* When I finish my detailed description of the meeting – I had to recall each name for my father, who thought he might have known most members – my mother says, "Did they seriously think you need a free meal?"

My father says he's happy I showed them I'm a real lady, with my choice of a cognac. Both of them then nod when I muse aloud that the only member to offer me food was the Jew among the Lions. Together we ponder this observation, but nobody has anything to add.

Later, as I re-live this evening in my mind, and with Geneva less than six months behind me, the Jewish student who took care of my friend Anita at the *Cité Universitaire* – this "Pouran from Iran" – comes to mind once again. Did she share something with Mr. Kagan that I don't know? Could it be, I ask myself, that the Jewish people, more than us Gentiles, have a special relationship with food? And why did Pouran even care about Anita and me like she did? The thought doesn't enter my mind that people can help others for no reason at all, even when they don't know each other.

In 2004, during a visit to Helsinki I go looking for Mr. Kagan's large storefront display on the *Boulevard*. Long gone, it isn't listed in the phone book either. I wonder if the picture of him with Marshall Mannerheim is still on display in the synagogue.

Americans And Their Questions

Even though I was a law student just back from independent studies in Geneva, my parents didn't allow me, or my sister, to date, at least not in the American way we saw Debbie Reynolds and Doris Day do on the white screen. Fortunately, I could occupy my mind with thoughts of the cute American boy I met in Switzerland. He was a law student at some university in Florida, a neutral topic that was useful for my letters to him. Except for the location of star-studded Miami Beach, I knew nothing about the state's geography so when he wrote about driving to the Keys (*what's a key?*) I didn't understand. His letters were also filled with stories about fraternity life (*Pi Kappa Alpha, what was that?*), and he repeated what he told me in Geneva about his blue Mustang convertible, his large rescue dog, and his now-divorced mother who'd moved to the port city of Savannah, Georgia; in that order. When he sent a picture of himself outside the fraternity house where he lived ("with a pool," as I told my mother), my sister said he resembled the Crown Prince of Sweden.

The following summer, 1966, I went to see him in Savannah. On the first night of my stay in his mother's shabby row-house in what Americans called a "mixed neighborhood," she invited me to sit on the porch with a glass of iced tea. After she shared her bitterness about a broken marriage that had resulted in her recent move to this cockroach-infested dwelling, which she said was the only place that would accept a pony-size mutt, she spoke of her son, who was nowhere in sight that night. He'd gone on the road selling encyclopedias so he could pay for his law school tuition.

While we waited for his unscheduled return from his latest travels, the mother erupted in a flood of anger about his girl-friend. "She's *Jewish*," she said as if describing a communicable affliction to this strange Scandinavian girl who'd just appeared by her front door.

I didn't understand why that was so terrible – visions of kind, unselfish "Pouran from Iran" passed through my head – but I was too intimidated by this corpulent lady to say anything. After a few days of her sputtering about her son dating this seemingly horrible Jew, and still waiting for the return of him (and whom I could barely remember any more), I finally collected myself after the surprise that my Geneva fellow was *dating* (leaving me a Doris Day movie character rejected by Rock Hudson). In my most formal British English I asked what made the girlfriend such a bad person. "Well, she's *Jewish* and we're not," said the mother.

Suddenly, all I wanted was to return to my familiar life in Helsinki, where I didn't know anybody angry about someone being Jewish.

Once at home, I spend my days moving robot-like between law classes and my study desk at the library. Only on weekends and holidays do I allow myself to do something different as I'd become a certified city guide for hordes of cruise passengers going on tours pre-set by my employer. Usually, they wax poetic about their first sight from the bow of their ship. Commonly nicknamed the White City of the North, Helsinki presents itself through the neoclassical Lutheran cathedral next to the gilded onion-domed Greek-Orthodox *Uspensky* Cathedral, both of them majestic on high enough elevations to be seen during the slow approach to the port. As long as I continue working as a tourist guide, they remain obvious stops on my city tours.

In the fall of 1967, a new point of interest is added: the Sibelius monument, dedicated to the iconic Finnish composer. Unfortunately, two other spectacular sites aren't built until after I leave my old life behind: the Rock Church built inside a gigantic slab of granite (1969), and the Finlandia Concert Hall designed by world famous Alvar Aalto in 1971.

Although the city had been severely bombed by the Soviets during the last war, the *Art Nouveau* style continues to be quite prominent in one interest-drawing place in particular: the main railway station (1919), which was Eliel Saarinen's last project before he emigrated to the US where Americans commonly associate the last name with his son, Eero (designer of the St. Louis Arch). Some will even bring up the name before I get around to it during a tour.

One day in the sightseeing bus, one of the male tourists asks for the mike. *How these Americans always must say something.*

"Wasn't General Mannerheim a hero to the Jews?" he wants to know.

This kind of probing into Finnish history happened so frequently that today I believe the largest number of my American tourists must have been Jewish, since none of my Scandinavian or German visitors ever asked about "anything Jewish," as I dutifully note in my diary. And there's definite reverence in their tone when they mention Mannerheim; no titles or first name needed for a wartime General of his repute.

They don't know he was a Swedish-speaking Finn, and moreover a notable aristocrat, but when I want to avoid an explanation of the whole Swedish-Finnish thing I say nothing about that. Instead, I give them touristy tidbits about the main thoroughfare in Helsinki, which still bears his name and where the eponymous *Marski* Hotel stands in a prime downtown location. Its main claim to fame when it was built in 1962 was that it housed the country's first night club. I also point out how he sits in parade-mode on his horse, the statue prominently placed by the main post office and today, the world-renowned main library.

While self-consciously posing for these inquisitive Americans with their ever-present peel-apart prints from the Polaroids around their necks, I only hope there won't be any questions that'd make me look uneducated and unsophisticated. The kind of English nuance needed for any additional discussion finally drives me to the Parliament Library, where I retrieve more facts on the Marshall (a military rank given the General in 1933).

The next time I get the question about him and the Jews, I confidently say, "Although he was uncomfortable with any accolades by the Jewish community, historians say he was a hero to the Jews because he openly disliked the Nazi leader."

When Hitler flew north to the Finnish army headquarters to honor Mannerheim on his 75th birthday, official protocol prevented him from being anything but cordial towards the Führer. Instead, in a show of what we might call passive aggression today, the aging General lit a cigar knowing quite well how the Chancellor of Nazi Germany didn't tolerate smokers around himself.

"Unfortunately, there's no record of how Hitler reacted to this social breach," I continue. "All we know for a fact is that his one and only visit to Finland on June 4, 1942 lasted five hours."

"Yes, but did he actually *do* something for the Jews?" someone is then likely to shout out.

This is where it gets tricky. Historians have dissected Mannerheim's memoirs (written in Swedish) and compared them to Finnish government records to understand if there ever was an official demand by the Nazis for the Jews in Finland and if Mannerheim played a role in "saving the Jews."

His cryptic comments, "[the] government decided to oppose German demands" shed little light on an issue that continues to be ripe with speculation. He also wrote, "My contribution … has been inconsiderable. I have done nothing more than what every person with a true sense of justice would be duty-bound to do."

As I mentioned before, somewhere in the Helsinki synagogue (built in 1906) is a photo of our wartime hero, Field Marshall and President Carl Gustaf Mannerheim, also named Liberator of Finland by the United States. Dated December 6, the Finnish Independence Day, 1944, the picture was taken at an event commemorating the 23 Jewish-Finnish soldiers who died for their country in the two recent wars against the Soviet Union. Much later, I'll read about one of the speakers at that occasion, Eliezer Berlinger, a rabbi from Sweden (soon-to-be chief rabbi of Finland), whose praise of Mannerheim included the congregation's gratitude for him having stood firm in "the fatal hour for Finland's Jewry." In 1960, he even got his own stamps as part of the Champions of Liberty series of the US Postal Service, but by then he'd passed away (in 1951).

With only the fuzzy recollection of a five-year old, I was told my father removed his hat as he stood with me and my sister solemnly watching the General's hearse being pulled across the Senate Square on its way to *Hietaniemi* (*Sandudd* in Swedish), the graveyard of all but two of the Finnish presidents. One portion of this huge park-like land, which includes a public beach serenely framed by the bay, is a separate area for Jewish war veterans and others of the Mosaic faith. At the edge of these grounds is the Chapel of the Crematorium.

Many decades later I'll contemplate the irony – or maybe it's just the poor judgment by city planners – of the location of the crematorium, open since 1926 to funerals of people of all faiths who've chosen to have their remains disposed of by fire. At the age of 17, I wrote in my journal about my nausea ("again") from the smell of a burning corpse coming from the *Krematoriekapellet*. When, in Miami, I learn about the protestations by German civilians living next door to a camp crematorium that they didn't know a thing about the killings, I know it's a lie.

By the time my parents pass away and their wishes for cremation are fulfilled, the smoke with its accompanying stench has been controlled by environmental regulations calling for natural gas to heat the ovens.

But back to Helsinki in the '60s. My interactions with Americans, real or celluloid, continued to feed my yearning for an exciting international career outside the confines of my home life in a country where I felt I didn't belong. I became obsessed with getting my law degree in the fastest way possible (at that time, the competition among students was to graduate "first" in terms of time, as opposed to making top grades). But when I wrote the United Nations headquarters in NYC to ask about my future job prospects, I received a curt response that, as a female, I should develop secretarial skills. My dejection was quickly forgotten when one of my law professors invited me to be a hostess at a convention of patent lawyers from around the world holding all their sessions at our law school. *Americans? From Santa Monica?* Once again, my imagination ran wild.

This was when a Mr. Gold from New Jersey befriended me. He was a short and lean, elderly gentleman with a gravelly voice that seemed to say he'd been a heavy smoker at one time. Visibly kind and considerate, he hesitated when he asked me to fulfill the usual hosting-duties of filling up pitchers of water, sharpening pencils, and fetching fresh cups of coffee for his committee members.

During a break he approached me, a concerned look on his face. "What's the standard of living of the Jews in Helsinki?" he asked.

I couldn't understand why he'd be interested in something like that but, dutifully, because I really wanted to please this affable man from America, I drew from my still limited knowledge.

"Oh, there are no starving Jews in Finland," I said nonchalantly, using the literal translation of what I'd heard others say. What I failed to add was that the social services provided by the state were such that nobody, regardless of religion or ethnicity, had to be without food or housing.

After the conference, we stayed in touch. He wrote about his wife and daughter, and their interest in sculpture and music. Later, they even send me a wedding gift. When they visit South Florida, my new husband and I invite them to dinner at our house in Miami. Anxious to serve something typical of where we settled, I slow-cook a Cuban-style ham overnight and serve it with the requisite *moros* and *platanitos*. They don't touch the pork.

As I clean off the table, Mrs. Gold apologizes. "My father was a rabbi, you know."

I have no idea how that'd make Jews eat differently. *Maybe it's just the American way of passing up food they don't like.* I'd been raised with post-war shortages that demanded we eat whatever was put in front of us. The only time the subject of Jews and their food had come up in our small-talk around the dinner table was when I balked over salt herring or mashed turnips; the worst was the lumpy oatmeal porridge, which grew what we called a "skin" if you let it sit too long. Rather than speaking of starving Africans, stories my contemporaries got at their homes, mother said to be grateful for all food because in the concentration camps Jews made broth out of leather belts. Much later, when I get to meet survivors in Miami and as co-travelers to Israel I'm embarrassed to mention my mother's soup-story. As far as I go, it only remains a loving incentive by her to make my young sickly self eat.

Bowling At The Hague

Historically, Scandinavians have treasured the long nights when the sun barely sets, giving them plenty of time to enjoy their modest summer cottages by the seashores and mountains. Maybe it's my determination to finish law school as soon as possible, or maybe a growing demand for my work as a tourist guide which means I finally have some money of my own, or maybe it has something to do with the unusually beautiful weather that summer of 1967 (climate change wasn't yet in anyone's vocabulary), but whatever it is, I'm in a high state of excitement as I pack for my upcoming trip to the Netherlands. Just months before, on a whim, I'd competed for a Dutch scholarship although the odds seemed insurmountable. There'd been three male applicants and all of them had gotten letters of recommendation from our international law professor who said he couldn't do the same for me because I was a "girl." Among these four contenders from Finland – and the only Swedish-speaking at that! – I'm now the winner.

Holland, here I come!

Since my parents left for the summer cottage as usual, I have the apartment to myself so I can plan every little detail for the upcoming trip. Convinced my prior "training" in aristocratic behavior will make me able to fake sophistication and worldliness among all the accomplished internationalists gathering at the same Hague program as I, I confidently lay out my dark-colored straight skirts and a few collared white blouses, and flats, along with one pair of fuchsia-colored long cotton pants for any sightseeing. An impulse makes me toss onto the modest pile my prized Sandra Dee-type sleeveless dress in blue gingham and with a flowing skirt. Although the family edict continues to scorch my ears – *Dignity above all* – I want to try out the merry ways of the girls in the Santa Monica movie from some years before.

Meanwhile, in the Land of the Midsummer Sun (Norway), Jon, the 23-year old grandson of a late Supreme Court Justice rummages through his Oslo apartment for the clothes he plans to wear during yet another trip to the continent. Since his family tree includes not only his distinguished grandfather, but the Justice's wife, Jon's grandmother and a leading advocate for women's rights, some would say Jon belongs to the highest social strata in his country. Like his famous grandfather, he's also chosen law as his professional career, although it'd take years until he too positions himself as a judge.

For now, he readies himself for a summer course at the mecca for diplomats and international law students from all around the world, the Hague Academy, where he, too, is determined not to let the books get the better of his time there. He's already planning to take some time off for the sandy beaches of *Scheveningen*, so unlike those on the rugged Norwegian coast.

Then, there's the bowling he loves.

"Holland, here I come," he says to himself as a mischievous thought enters his mind. The big poster of Mao on his living room wall is calling for him to toss his "chairman's jacket" into the suitcase, but he changes his mind. He'll need that space for his bowling pants and shirts.

On a balmy Monday afternoon in July, at the *Vredespaleis* (the palace-like building often called the seat of international law) where the renowned Hague Academy was housed, students crowd the exits after dismissal as each contemplates what to do next. Those attendees overhearing someone speak their own language congregate around each other. I, a Swedish-speaking Finn, look around for other fellow "Scandihoovians" as we Scandinavians jokingly call each other. When I hear two Danes in a huddle with three Norwegians, all of them male, I spontaneously approach the little clique.

Så roligt att höra hemlandstoner (how nice to hear voices from home), I say to nobody in particular, knowing very well that my accented Swedish is a give-away for my national origin.

One of the Norwegians swings around with a big grin. "Hurrah, a Finn who actually speaks Swedish so I can understand you! … we were just talking… want to go bowling?" he says.

"Yes! I'll show you how a *real* Viking woman beats a Norseman." I'm surprised and pleased at how easy it's to be jocular with strangers. Of the male variety, no less.

It isn't until we're on our way to the bowling alley that I confess I've never been in one.

"With your athletic looks you'll pick up the game in no time. There's nothing to worry about," he says.

And, that's when a life-long friendship is born between Jon and myself.

When I show up for our next bowling session, he compliments me on my baby-blue gingham dress (*Sandra Dee, you should see me now!*) but says pants are more practical. When I fret about shoes, he tells me about getting them at the alley. If my mother only knew: *renting* shoes – whoever heard of such a thing for our family? – and *bowling* with a man! I can picture her raising one eyebrow in the usual gesture of disapproval.

Jon is a natural storyteller, weaving little snippets of his own political beliefs (Chairman Mao figures prominently) with social nuggets (particularly, lack of gender equality, which, according to his vehement assertions, should already have been eliminated in Scandinavia). Our exchanges mostly take place in the bowling alley or on the beaches of *Scheveningen*, both places not conducive to any serious history lessons or substantive subject matters. Twenty-one years after WWII ravaged both of our countries, our generation is busy looking ahead. We don't want to talk about the past, including the German occupation of Norway or the wartime Jewish Question in his home country or mine.

But when I mention how, on my way down to the Hague, I spent one night at an Amsterdam youth hostel named after Anne Frank, he says, "Then you must have seen the rooms where she and her family hid from the Nazis."

Reluctantly, I admit I hadn't included it in my city tour and, although I'd read Anne's diary in its Swedish translation from 1953, I know little about the larger context of her internment. And even less about the deportation of Norwegian Jews to concentration camps, a subject he mentions in passing but then quickly drops as he sees my lack of reaction. Still, and without me noticing it, he becomes my contemporary window to the twice-removed Nordic neighbor (Sweden is, after all, situated between his country and mine). I particularly like it when we compare our lives in not only two geographically close but otherwise divergent countries, but also in families that couldn't have been more different. His grandfather, Thomas Bonnevie, was a Supreme Court Justice during part of the occupation, and I can also see how animated he becomes when talking about his grandmother Margarete, wife of the Justice and a leader in the nascent suffragist movement in Norway. My own grandparents, farmers and small businessmen all, were so mundane in comparison. Still, the women were strong in their own way and I don't recall anyone ever talking about lacking any rights.

It'll take more than four decades, which include my move to America, before I press Jon on his recollections about the salient years in Norway. This I'll do purely with selfish motives when my usual fear of looking ignorant drives me to learn how to face a continuous stream of questions about the overall area of Scandinavia, not just Finland, during WWII. Later in the book, I'll share how I integrate these facts in my talks.

On the first day of classes, a sense of familiarity had drawn me into the circle of fellow Scandinavians. But it's also the day I spotted *Him*.

In his madras sports jacket and with a narrow, conservative tie he might as well have carried a sign, *I'm American.* When he asked me to meet him later in the evening at a particular club at *Scheveningen,* the historical seaside resort of the Hague, I had to remind myself I already had an earlier bowling date with Jon. Did I really have the courage to go out a second time on the same day? Would that make me into the whore mother had called me when she secretly watched me, at age16, getting kissed on the cheek by a German male visitor?

Imagine *me* now, being asked by this handsome American, who with his resemblance to Bobby Kennedy and impeccable manners spelled class and royalty. Americans may not have had their own aristocracy, but this fellow student came close.

From then on, my double life began. When classes were dismissed in the afternoon I went bowling with Jon, only to have to rush home to change for my evening dates with *Him.* When he said, "You're a real lady," I knew he recognized me for the class I thought an American sophisticate like he admired. Just like in the scenes in the Santa Monica movies, I, too, was now wanted. Dizzy from the unfamiliar flirtatiousness that was a manifestation of my new freedom, I didn't yet understand why other classmates got angry when I rejected their advances. When a German student asked me to a dance, I was incensed. Imagine someone like him, in sandals and socks, asking someone like *me*!

Before the program ended and everyone returned to their home countries, *He* invited me to come to America to visit him and his parents for Christmas. The mail from him – at that time, few people made transatlantic telephone calls – was so intense (sometimes three letters in a day) that not only my mother and father commented on it, but so did our mailman who called him "relentless."

One day in the fall when I was back in my routine of nothing else but memorizing statutory provisions needed for spewing them up on some law school exam or the other, and mother seemed in a relaxed mood, I talked about going overseas once again. That *He* had invited me to meet his parents for a family holiday made it all seem so legitimate, so high-class, so promising.

"If you can come up with the money yourself, you may go," mother said in a flat voice, knowing very well I didn't have enough.

My father refused to talk about it at all, not even uttering the name of my American prince. My sister and I spoke of "acting royal" again, and we spent hours scrutinizing my wardrobe – just in case. My brother, by then a practicing attorney, surprised me with an offer to assist him with an estate inventory, for which I was paid half of the cost of my airline fare. I made up the remainder by baby-sitting.

Although mother had no point of reference for what constituted "society" in America, she was in high spirits when I returned home with elaborate stories about my visit with the family of *Him*, my Bobby Kennedy stand-in. Probably because he was the only Catholic we knew, that made him unique in a curious sort of way. And, when described in Swedish, the Polish-Ukrainian roots of his parents sounded aristocratic or at least continental. Never mind, my chatter about our future (*did he actually propose during my visit with his family*? I was never certain I understood him correctly) was fueled by my persistent desire to get away from home. I'd already begun counting the days till I'd be the wife of *Him* who wooed me that fateful, previous summer in Holland.

One week before the wedding, I graduated. The first in my class to do so, exactly as I'd planned on my schedule. There was no formal ceremony; we only shook hands with the dean (or "rector" as he was called) and then I slogged through the wintry December-landscape of Helsinki to get home, where my father had a piece of French pastry waiting for me. Mother was on her bed, groaning about one leg with its augury of a looming blood clot.

There hadn't been any discussion about where the marriage ceremony was to take place: The German Lutheran Church around the corner from my first childhood home. Popular for its small size and its quaint red bricks and tall steeples, the century-old sanctuary had long been the preferred wedding venue for the Swedish elite. It was the only place for me, too.

His parents asked for a priest from the only Catholic church in Helsinki to give a blessing at the service, and when they learned clergy from that congregation wouldn't set foot in a Protestant church, they simply renamed their son's wedding site something more Catholic-sounding ("St. John's," to be exact) in the notice they later sent to the social pages of their local paper. When

I told my father I already felt rejected by my in-laws-to-be, he said what he usually did when I was hurt by someone's actions, "Just laugh it off; don't take things so seriously."

The sun had already set on the wintry Friday afternoon in December 1968 when I became the wife of my American prince, who continued to evoke images of royalty through his gentlemanly demeanor alone. I was his princess in my faux-pearl crown, which held in place a short tulle veil that capped off my white "princess-style"-dress, quite fashionable at the time, although made by me from a German *Burda* pattern and fitted with the help of a cousin.

In the presence of less than twenty guests I said my Protestant vows in Swedish, while *He* responded in English. His mother, looking so "American" in her above-the-knee, baby-blue dress with a tiny matching hat made of the same silk, wiped away her tears. His father was on his knees in whispered prayer.

In the true, hostile sibling-format my brother had long been using against his two sisters, he refused to tell me if he'd be the best-man. It wasn't until I arrived at the church that I saw him by the altar.

And, till the morning of the wedding I also didn't know if mother would attend. A few months earlier she'd "warned" me – her words to *prepare* me, as she said – she wasn't sure she'd make it to the ceremony because of some anticipated illness, which might lead to her passing away (one of her many deaths through the years). If it weren't for my American in-laws, before whom mother had to maintain the high-class demeanor that characterized people like us, she wouldn't be sacrificing her own wellbeing. So, there she was, covering her small but full figure in a custom-tailored dress and jacket, made of some drab jacquard-type cloth frequently favored by Eastern European women. For the first time in a long while, probably years, she'd applied a touch of color on her tightly pursed, disciplined lips.

Filled with guilt over the work and extra expense I'd caused my parents by insisting on a church wedding, tiny as it was even by the then-standards of Finland, I was desperate to have it all behind me. Kneeling next to my American prince for the final marriage blessing, with Jesus looking down at me from the large crucifix in the painting high above the altar, I fervently offered my silent plea. *Please God, help me be a good wife but first, get me away from here.*

After a honeymoon at the luxury resort *Son Vida* in Mallorca – how *royal* was that! – I was ready for my new life. Just after midnight on January 2, 1969 it began. It wasn't Santa Monica, but it *was* America.

Part 2
The Furr'ner

As the doors to the DC-8 swung open I wanted to inculcate myself with the air of my new hometown: Birmingham, Alabama. It smelled nothing like the lingering bus fumes I knew from Helsinki or the musky brackishness of its harbor where I played as a child. But neither was it like what my sister and I'd considered an "American smell," something we couldn't pinpoint when we first encountered it in gift packages from visiting emigrants to "Amerika." In my letters home, I'll now be describing it as a mix of root beer and Chiclet gum.

My chest heaved as my breathing deepened. The captivity of my old environment that had seemed so oppressive before suddenly turned to a longing for the familiar safety I'd left behind.

My husband interrupted my reminiscing. "Look at that, honey," he said with only a slight slur from a long night of transcontinental enjoyment of Dewar's White Label. "They're all out there waiting to greet you..., everyone's curious to meet my new bride from Finland."

Me? Why would anyone want to meet me? Those Americans really are something else.

And then I saw them: the swarm of a handful of impeccably coiffed, fur-wrapped Southern Belles in their mid-20's, balancing on high heels as they raced across the tarmac towards the plane. They were the wives and girlfriends of my husband and his law school classmates, who'd already enlisted him, a Yankee by birth but a Southerner by choice, for their long-established country club circles. Later that evening, one of them took me aside. "If ya'll hadn't gotten your hands on him, we'd have kept him to ourselves," she said.

But now, still peering through the small airplane window, I shuddered from what lay silently in the air: the intimidation of the waiting contemporaries who, in just a few seconds will pass judgment on this creature from Finland whom, I was sure, they didn't recognize as high-class Swedish-Finnish blood. An intruder on their territory, she wore a steel-blue A-line coat (*bless her little heart, it's* cloth!) with a narrow white mink collar (*poor thing, such a* small *fur!*), matching blue leather boots (*the dear girl mustn't know enough to know one travels in heels*) and a white mink pillbox hat on top of her crumpled blond bun (*oh my, do those Scandinavians... or is she Swiss?... still carry on about that Yankee, Jackie Kennedy? My, my... does her husband* really *know what he got himself into?*).

"Hi ya'll!" He shouted from the open platform of the plane. "Ya'll here for us?"

I straightened my back, raised my chin high and assumed my well-honed royal posture. My right hand went up in a wave perfected through years of daydream and practice. Like the British Queen, I clutched a small purse to my side as I regally descended into my new life.

It didn't take long for the buzz to begin among the country club matrons. "He married a furr'ner," they said about my American husband. The tone of their voices was that of someone alarmed over the unfamiliar. One night, balancing gin and tonic refills, one of the young Belles said without any sign of embarrassment at all how much she just *hated* Negroes, Catholics, Jews, and "furr'ners." I wasn't black, Catholic or Jewish but I fit right into her last group of vilified people, although the Southern Baptists, as I was to learn later, were quick to add they had nothing against other kinds of people. "Just the *sinners*."

Silently I reflected on my experience in Geneva and the Hague when a fellow student who came from another country was a person of instant interest. Here in Birmingham, I'd already been declared a Southern bane.

Another of the Belles knew of a local Finnish girl whom she wanted me to meet. I balked.

By rote, I told her, "I'm really a *Swedish* Finn…; our language is Swedish, you know."

She gave me a blank stare. Swiss, Swedish, Finnish, Russian…, it was all the same to these country-clubbers.

Adding to the dilemma of who I was, at least in my new social circles, was the matter of hyphenated Americans; immigrants who insisted on showing their heritage by adding their nationality of origin to their new citizenship. Should I then be Finnish with a hyphen, but, if so, what came first, the Swedish or the Finnish part? Was I a Swedish-Finn or Finnish-Swede? A Swede-Finn or a Finn-Swede? In Swedish we still call ourselves *finlandssvenskar*, one word that says it all but doesn't translate into English in a way that those transplants to America could agree on. It'd take intense deliberations by members of the Swedish Finn Historical Society in Seattle before an official moniker was finally selected: "Swedish Finn." No hyphen wanted or needed.

Would Americans understand any of this? Would it help me decide who I was? In later desperation, I took to telling people, "I'm Swedish but born in Finland," but that didn't solve anything either. Mortified over having drawn attention to myself with those words– an unacceptable flaunting of myself – I ended up crawling back to the familiar silence of being on the outside looking in.

Soon, my husband's friends were wondering why his bride was so detached. Perhaps I didn't know English? What they didn't know was that the language of the Deep South wasn't at all like the Queen's English that was mandatory in both my middle and high school. But then there was also what I'd come to believe was an indigenous characteristic among Americans, one that I couldn't even try to emulate: the way their words tumbled freely and frequently from their mouths, without any apparent forethought or discernible pauses. Long before my arrival in Birmingham, lips had already been flapping. In his letters, my husband-to-be had described in great detail the curiosity of his friends when he spoke about me. That had made me spend sleepless nights worrying about living up to expectations I knew I couldn't fulfill. In my journal I only hinted at my anxieties when I wrote, "Those Americans are so *unreal*" and, "If things don't work out, I'll just have to get a divorce." As if the latter even was an acceptable option in a family like mine.

But there I was now, in the Deep South, married to someone who at least reminded me of royalty. So, why did I still feel like I was doomed to living on the outside?

A year after the establishment of our first married home we left Birmingham – in April 1970, to be exact – for the burgeoning international city of Miami, Florida. There, two sons are born, and my old home country appoints me its local consular representative, a position that inherently comes with a lot of prestige and public curiosity but little financial reward.

The Yellow Star That Wasn't

Determined to be content with living through *Him*, my American hero with the impeccable manners, I settled into our new life in Miami where we didn't know even one person. He was one of four new associates in a downtown law firm and these then became our first friends. One of them, in retrospect I think he was Jewish (although at the time it wasn't anything I thought about), soon brought up the subject of the wartime King of Denmark. "Christian X was good to the Jews," he said. "In solidarity with them, he wore the Yellow Star, you know."

I squirmed. "I'm from *Finland*," I said, as if this justified my ignorance.

Thanks to the Web, most of us know today that a story like that about the Danish king is fictional, a legend easily dismissed in the context of verifiable, historical facts. Still, it makes me wonder. Since they managed to live on for so long, they must have gotten started somewhere. If I dug some more, was there perhaps a tiny grain of truth somewhere?

Decades before the English-language edition of Leon Uris's *Exodus* first appeared in 1958, a Jewish man named Edward Bernays was born in Vienna, Austria (interestingly, the nephew of Sigmund Freud). As a one-year old child he moved with his family to America, where he lived to be 103. At his own request, his obituary lists him as the "Father of Spin," something that's relevant to the royal myth, even though he unfortunately took with him to his grave whatever he knew about the origin and spread of the tale about King Christian X.

Although there's no absolute proof it was Bernays who invented the story about the king and the Jewish star, he's also gone down in history as the creator of public relations. As such, he was paid at least once as a "consultant" to the Friends of Danish Freedom and Democracy, a group of Danish nationals operating from the US offices of the National Denmark-America Association. Whether a propaganda bulletin or just an informative newsletter put out by the organization sharing the same mission as the Danes back home, The *Danish Listening Post* has his fingerprints all over it. "Manipulation of public opinion is a necessary part of democracy" is how he justified his lifelong efforts for the causes in which he believed, and Denmark's image was one of them.

Another possible origin for the many stories about how Christian X sought to protect the Jews is a small photo of him in the *Washington Post*, dated November 22, 1942. Some sources believe that because the caption implied he willingly gave his country to Hitler, it later inspired the National Denmark-America Association to join with Jewish organizations to hold a support rally in Madison Square Garden in NYC in 1943. By that time, there were reliable reports about the Nazis tightening their controls over Denmark so a large gathering of supporters wouldn't only raise necessary funds for setting the record straight on the situation, but it would also draw attention to the dangers the Danish Jews were facing. Although the *Post* had previously had a small item about the upcoming event, there was still no mention of any behind-the-scenes directions by the public relations expert himself. Regardless, the "real truth" about Denmark had to be told, even when it meant it had to be invented, and even possibly with the help of a spin doctor like Bernays.

There was certainly plenty of fodder for "spinning" the actions of the royal leaders of the geographically obscure area called Scandinavia, where reindeer were still reported to roam and kings and queens were written about fairytale-like as if they were above reproach. Additionally, the American public was commonly confused by a complex royal family tree dating back to Queen Victoria of England, with Denmark and Norway being ruled by two brothers, and the daughter of the King of Sweden married to the Danish crown prince. The only Nordic country not a kingdom, was Finland (after the First World War, the offer of a Finnish throne had been made to a German prince, who turned it down).

When, one week after the German invasion of Denmark in 1940, a little princess was born in Copenhagen this was the kind of good news that public relations professionals could use to shine a rosy light on a country, which had already been widely criticized for not resisting the invasion by Hitler. Thirty-two years later, the baby princess went on to ascend to the Danish throne as Queen Margrethe. About the ongoing debate of the heroism of her grand-father King Christian X, she's had this to say: "The truth is an even greater honor for our country than the myth." For me, those words have done nothing to clarify the facts. I'm still left to wonder about the king's presumed heroism in the face of what the Nazis generally called the Jewish Question.

It would take me till 2013 to shed more light on the "did he or didn't he" dilemma.

That year, I came across the reprint of an old cartoon from January 10, 1942 in a trade and maritime journal from *Sweden*, not Denmark, by the sketch-artist, Ragnvald Blix, a native of *Norway*. Since he already had a reputation for publicly sharing his anti-Fascist feelings he must have been quite pleased to have this presumably neutral venue to express himself (although Sweden had made a formal declaration of neutrality, we'll see later why it earns no stars for its partisan activities during the war).

In this occupation-time drawing, the Danish king is deep in conversation with his prime minister. The caption says, "What shall we do, Your Majesty, if [the head of the government] says our Jews also have to wear yellow stars?"

Says the king, "Then we'll probably all wear the Yellow Star."

Today, we know this is based on an actual conversation, recorded in the king's handwritten notes and journals made accessible to a renowned Danish historian and other researchers long after the king's death in 1947.

Among those records is another direct quote from the king's personal journal: "If such a demand [towards the Jews] is made, we would best meet it by all wearing the Star of David."

While these newly discovered facts back up the legend about the Yellow Star in Denmark, the story in the children's book of the same name and in both the *Exodus* narratives (book and movie), remains a myth. The king's resolve was simply never put to a test by the Germans.

Still, the authors of the above books may have been on to something. What if mythical tales like these fulfill a real human need? Throughout history we've used allegories to re-calculate our moral compasses, so why shouldn't we welcome repetitions in books and movies? Some people have said if we successfully continue to "spin" the story about the Jewish star in Denmark it might inspire us to take action against the human rights violators of today, although history shows us no spinning of the facts is needed when telling the Danish story.

Regardless, myths tend to live on. Maybe better to call them partial truths when they come with historical nuances leading to verifiable facts. Among the most persistent statements I hear is that "all" Danish Jews disappeared into safety *overnight*. People often believe this magic was made possible by Sweden eagerly waiting to take them in. A lovely story, fit for a children's book. But the truth is that around the time of the planned deportation in the fall of 1943, the Swedish attitude towards the Danish Jews was unknown. At least in theory, early refugees could have been turned away when they reached land in Sweden.

Already in 1942, though without any official policy statements, Sweden had closed its doors to Jews from *Finland*, calling their admission a "sign of weakness" [on Finland's part]. Swedish government officials didn't even relent when a representative of the World Jewish Congress made a personal appeal in Stockholm; they just continued holding firm to the decision that "nothing should be done [for the Jews from Finland] unless the situation got worse." Since Jewish refugees from Norway had already been turned away, who was to say those fleeing Denmark wouldn't face the same fate?

It'd take a year for Sweden to clarify where it stood on its policy on the Danish Jews. Specifically, it was a matter of agreeing on how to proceed. In 1943, Duckwitz, a German diplomat in Copenhagen, made a formal appeal to the Swedish government that Danish Jews be received by Sweden. Although the response was affirmative, it came with the condition that this arrangement be approved by the Nazis. Historians now claim the request was simply ignored by Germany, resulting in total inaction. The question therefore remained, would Sweden admit or not admit Jews who were lucky enough to safely make it to Swedish shores? Nobody knew. At the same time, something was happening in the major war arena to force the hand of the supposedly neutral government of Sweden. That "something" was far away, in the south of the Soviet Union.

When Hitler's efforts to extend his *Lebensraum* to the east ended with his failure to capture the strategically vital city of Stalingrad in February 1943, the world took this as a sign that an Allied victory was certain. It also became the turning point for the Swedish government to consider its wartime image once peace was declared. How would the world look at a self-proclaimed neutral country that had continued trading with Germany, a nation determined to exterminate the Jewish population? Despite close emotional and historical ties between the Swedish royal house and Germany, Sweden wanted to be on the winning side that now seemed less and less likely to be the Reich. The two citizens, who came to play a major part in saving its reputation, were Raoul Wallenberg (with his safe passes) and Count Folke Bernadotte (with his Red Cross buses).

Before the Swedes finally adopted a public policy on Danish Jews escaping to Sweden, there was a man in Copenhagen with the brilliant mind of a scientist: the respected physicist Niels Bohr. In September 1943, he learned the German occupiers, while considering him Jewish (Scandinavian sources often paint him as half-Jewish since only his mother was of that faith), mainly looked at him as a prize in the race between the Allies and the Nazis for the atom bomb. When the final order for the roundup came down on Denmark, and with an invitation to become a contributing member of the Los Alamos team in the United States, he was secretly whisked off to Sweden on September 29, 1943. But Swedish officials and the American scientists who were looking forward to meeting this Dane who'd privately met with Werner Heisenberg, the German scientist known for his work on the atomic bomb, were in for a surprise. Bohr announced he was staying put in Sweden till its government announced that Danish Jews would be welcomed there. Some sources say he "demanded" that the policy be broadcast on Swedish radio (by the king, no less) and printed by the media. Whatever the real facts, the outcome of Bohr's temporary stay in Sweden was that on October 2, the king took to the airwaves to announce that the borders were open to all Jewish refugees from Denmark.

While the top-secret Manhattan atomic project, led by Robert Oppenheimer, was awaiting the arrival of the famous Danish physicist, he faced another – more personal – trial than demanding of Sweden a safe place for his compatriots. This one involved a basic understanding of the science behind airplanes. Although he'd been given an oxygen mask for the high-speed high-altitude flight to Scotland (the first stop on his way to America), his flight-helmet didn't fit him (no surprise to me, as I looked at pictures of him and marveled over his large, oval-shaped head, which I still think is often native to the people I remember from my childhood). Without it, he couldn't hear the intercom instructions for when to turn on the vital oxygen, so he promptly passed out. If he hadn't come to when the aircraft descended to lower altitudes, the Los Alamos atomic project might have been one scientist short of success. Although Oppenheimer credited him for clarifying what long remained a "stubborn puzzle," Bohr himself said later that the bomb would've been made without his help. After the war ended in 1945, he returned to Copenhagen, where he was a revered Dane and scientist till his death in 1962.

To this day, much speculation remains over Bohr's meeting in 1941 with Heisenberg. In 1998, I was at the National Theatre in London where the long-running play *Copenhagen* guesses at the subject under discussion by these two renowned scientists, both also students of philosophy. Their talk about war and morality gave me flashbacks of a play I'd seen as a teenager out of touch with the vicissitudes of history.

It was in January, 1964, on the stage of the historic Swedish Theatre in Helsinki that a new drama by the German playwright Rolf Hochhut was performed for the first time in Finland; naturally, in Swedish (the Finnish National Theatre did its own selections). Headlined as the *Stellverträter* (in my diary I use the German, not the Swedish, title for what became both the *Representative* and the *Deputy* in the English translation), the play raises the question whether Pope Pius XII could have prevented the transportation of Jews. Perhaps I didn't understand that conflict, because I don't remember many papal details, just the nauseating horror from seeing the background clips of dying camp inmates. As I wrote in my journal, at the end of the performance the already-silent audience stood to exit without a sound. "There was no applause whatsoever during or after the play," I recorded. What I had no way of knowing then was how controversial this Holocaust drama turned out to be wherever it was showing; later that year, the Broadway producer said he'd release any actors who felt they couldn't be part of the production.

When at the turn of the new century, I see in the deep bowels of my bookcases *Hitler's Pope* which examines the role of Pius XII in the slaughter of the Jews, the debilitating stomach cramps I remember from my first visual introduction in 1964 to doomed and dead Jews return. Mother may have been right about me all along. My queasiness over human misery would have made me unfit to become a doctor.

On The Outside

Now in my new life in Miami, I continued to question the consequences of fitting in, an ongoing conflict carried over from my teens. When I look through my journals from that part of my Finnish life, I see long periods of dread over what kind of person I should be. But did I really *want* to fit in, or was my life easier when lived in a daydream? Maybe it was just an illusion my life would be better if I were part of a group.

While I'd inherited a strong tendency towards separateness and individual direction, I didn't know how to reconcile it with familial or societal behavior, and I wondered if anybody else was as incapable of fulfilling expectations. Much later, long after I settled in America, I read somewhere that the rituals for acceptance by the Nordic society are as baffling to the uninitiated as those for Hasidic Jews. And then I don't feel quite as much of an outsider.

But then, enter Paul Newman onto my internal stage. Correctly as Ari Ben, his character in the movie *Exodus*, which my husband and I had recently checked out at the Blockbuster store. Even though I'd seen the film before, it suddenly seemed he was talking directly to me when he said people want to be the same. Or, as a Jewish camp survivor later reminisced in a documentary about his reluctance to visit the Berlin of his birth, "It's painful to be different."

When I first became a mother in Miami, today's concept of "celebrating differences" wasn't a part of anyone's parlance. Mostly, I saw the same kind of women who I believed had judged me so harshly in Birmingham, decked out in their appliqued skirts and carrying painted wooden purses in the shape of miniature houses. With hair sprayed stiff, not a strand out of place, they seemed to ooze the high social standing of an ideal I could never achieve. And I knew I had to remain different. For my sake.

Till one day, for some inexplicable reason, I decided I had to do something for the benefit of my school-aged sons. Since "everybody's" mother seemed to belong to the same association, the Junior League, I completed an application fully expecting to become one of "them." When I was told I was ineligible because I was foreign-born (*could it be they didn't want to use the Birmingham moniker of "furr'ner?"*), I accepted my fate of remaining a bystander.

But then there was Cotillion, the traditional group for young teens to learn social dances and good manners. Both of my sons wanted to do what their peers did.

My role as a mother in this group seemed uncomplicated enough. I was only asked to provide the occasional cookie tray, although even a simple task like that made me feel like a permanent outsider when one of the mothers corrected my placement of the goodies (vanilla cookies had to be in a row with all other vanillas, and chocolate with chocolate). Then, she pointedly asked if I was "legacy." I'm convinced it was because I made the social *faux pas* of asking her what it meant I was never called on again. Birmingham or Miami, the social structure was still bewildering for someone like me.

Through my sons' school and after-school activities, my circles slowly widened to mostly Jewish women although their self-assurance, style, and poise intimidated me just as much as the Belles of Birmingham had. Moreover, groups of women had long made my stifling fear of criticism rise to the surface. So, when the mother of a classmate of my fifth-grade son invited me to her synagogue, Temple Judea, for what was billed as an Interfaith Day I didn't want to go. What could I possibly learn that I didn't already know from years of mandatory religion classes in Finland? Besides, what made this mother think I was the least interested in comparing Judaism with Catholicism and Protestantism? Mentally, I had plenty of excuses but, as usual, I remained silent. The mother counted on me, but she didn't have to know I was an unwilling guest.

While I was fighting these internal struggles, wordlessly alone, my married life continued to glide by like in the illusionary aristocratic households where servants smoothly and inconspicuously tend to their masters, freeing them from the burden of having to face themselves. *Dignity at any cost*.

In October of 1988, a judge in Miami told my American prince and me in open court with our two sons in attendance, that she wished all divorces were as friendly as ours, but when I looked at the final decree I sobbed. In a letter from my mother, but with obvious traces of my sister's voice, she said it came as no surprise that my husband, whom she hadn't asked about in ten years of hostile letters to me, *left* someone like me.

"A pushy mother and now, as we've learned, a no-good wife. I wouldn't want to be a dog in your house."

From my father, not a word.

B e s h e r t

It was the end of Yom Kippur, the holiest of all Jewish holidays. Across America, Jews were breaking fast together as I stood in the foyer of my friend's house in Miami. I felt envy creeping up on me as family after family arrived for the bountiful table of traditional holiday foods. Five years into my divorced life I had nobody. My sons were away in college and my parents lived across the ocean. Utterly alone, I was a silent but committed spectator of a life I never had. A Lutheran by birth, an Episcopalian by choice, I was completely surrounded by only Jews with families, all of them united by their traditions.

Suddenly, a *Brioni* stepped across the threshold. The man who wore it looked to be around 60 with a slightly slumped posture making the fashionable Italian suit seem incongruent not only with his physique but also with his lop-sided grin that hinted at whimsy. Later I'd see Victor Borge in his face and a wave of reassuring familiarity would roll over me.

In a physical sense he was not a classically handsome man, although his friends described him as such. They also said he was loyal and generous and with a great affinity for a good joke. He was about 5'11" in height and had a perfectly groomed, full head of gray hair. A strong fragrance of cologne made it seem as if he tried to assert himself by scent alone. His eyes were the bluest of blue, with little crinkles suggesting a man in perpetually good spirits. Gold-rimmed glasses made him look maturely bookish, in stark contrast to the palpable aura of innocence like that of a child who was still discovering the world around him. In an instant, I wanted to put my arms around him to shield him from all the evil people in the universe, but fortunately the deep-seated familiar insecurities intervened.

Although American clothing manufacturers wanted me to believe I was a "Medium Petite," I'd long felt plump and pudgy. My upper arms were proportionately too heavy, so I hadn't gone sleeveless for decades. My face was much too animated and frequently got me in trouble when people projected whatever they wished onto it. Mercifully, being blond and blue-eyed often fed into the common picture of what a typical Scandinavian should look like. Usually that elicited some compliments although it took years of living in America to fake graceful acceptance of them. Praise was non-existent in my old world, even for a goody-two-shoe, straight-A student like me.

"With your high forehead you look intelligent," was the closest my mother had come to praising her youngest child. But I'd wanted to look like Doris Day or some other American movie star who maintained her virginity with great self-confidence, but always won the heart of the most handsome man. When my first boyfriend, my now-ex, called me pretty I was instantly suspicious. Why would he say a thing like that? Did he say it to every girl? Was this part of a sexist romancing process with Americans?

A touch of an accent, often confused with British or German, had been a continued source of unreserved attention in my new home country causing me to feel the burden of my ancestral "mustn't stand out." Sometimes I responded with made-up stories to put an end to the curious questioning and at other times I assumed the self-effacing manner of an outsider who didn't miss an opportunity to diminish or make fun of herself.

But here I was now, silent and bashful, glancing at a *Brioni* stubbornly filling the entrance of the house. The distance to where I was standing was a mile long, or more like a foot and a half. I had nowhere to run. When Andy stepped forward to introduce himself, I froze in place.

Suddenly, a scarlet neon sign flashed from my forehead: "She's just fallen in love with that man!"

How could that be? Things like this weren't supposed to happen to me, an independent Scandinavian, a self-sufficient. . . .

The dreadful tape in my brain was relentless.

You idiot. You must be going crazy. Get a grip on yourself. Everyone is watching.

It took all my willpower to feign the calm that my heart didn't allow, and I resumed the posture of someone used to attending a lot of social events. I told myself, it would soon be over, and life could return to the comfortable solitude of singleness. Meanwhile, I could mingle with the people I already knew. As always, things would be fine. But they weren't. I remained transfixed, staring at Andy's outstretched hand as if it were both prophetic and ominous for the power it already had over me.

"So, I hear you're from Helsinki," he said so softly I had to lean in to catch his words. There was a trace of what I thought was a New York accent in the way he rolled his r's although much later I learned he'd left his hometown of Philadelphia more than thirty years earlier to manage the Florida arm of the family investment business. By then I also knew he was divorced with one grown daughter still living in "Philly," where he continued to go on regular visits to see her or his elderly parents and one older, married brother.

"Hmm, Helsinki," he said, as if pondering something. "That makes you Finnish."

After what seemed like an eternity, I managed to shake his out-stretched hand. The grip of his gentle smile made me stutter, "Yes, I g-guess so."

But then, in another flash of self-consciousness and with a self-serving effort to discomfit him I found my formal voice to say, "Actually, I'm a *Swedish* Finn. And I'm not *Jewish*."

It was love that brought Andy and me together, or at least that's what friends used to say. I believed in something even deeper than that, something that has to do with faith and things that are pre-destined. At the *Cygnaeus* Elementary School in Helsinki - an exclusive Swedish institution, named after a pioneering educator in Finland – we'd started each day with a hymn, frequently one with a favorite stanza of mine; about joy or pain that's *beskärt* (an archaic Swedish word used for the things God bestows on us, good or bad, deserved or not). When Andy described our meeting as *beshert*, I was transported right back to my childhood with a God who understood my agony over not fitting in.

Now, more than 30 years later, I had Andy telling me there was a place for me: *beskärt* or *beshert*, from two different languages but pronounced the same; it didn't matter. Either way, the Jewish expression was in itself a sign of the unseen force that brought the two of us together at the same event.

Or maybe it was just love, that inexplicable concept that only makes sense to the people experiencing it. Some quantum physicists have tried to explain it through an intricate formula of invisible particles vibrating at the same level, unbeknownst to the people attracted to each other. Others use the five senses to define love. It may be a physical attraction that establishes what they think is love, or the way someone talks or moves, or perhaps a combination of all sensory experiences. The point is there's no universal definition of love. It's unique to all.

My first experience with love was as a second grader in Helsinki. The boy at the wooden two-student desk behind me had big brown eyes and matching dark hair and when he pulled my scraggly blond braids, I felt special. Best of all, he did the forbidden: he laughed. A lot.

When he got a bike, I was lost in strange feelings of affection. The storybook prince of my future had quickly been replaced by a classmate with wheels. I saw a new world and I wanted to be part of it. When I told my parents, my mother got a dark look, the one I'll later recognize as a teenager when the subject of sex comes up.

Her tone had a reprimanding edge to it when she said, "*Who* do you think you are?"

But my father said, "Why don't you write him a letter?" So I did. I told the boy that we'd be married one day and that I, too, will have a bike. For days I saw only hope but when the boy never mentioned the letter, my mother said, "I told you it was silly." My eyes hurt from the tears of humiliation.

My father, in his usual way when he wanted to comfort me, said, "By the time you're a bride, you'll be fine."

But I wasn't. The shame was already etched deep into me. Years passed till, one day during a visit back to Helsinki, I watched my second-grade love object tenderly touching another classmate of mine as he guided her across the street. People passing by cast surreptitious looks at the young lovers who had the audacity to show affection in public. My cheeks burned like the multi-colored, tiled stoves that had kept our classroom warm in the winter. I lowered my head so they wouldn't see me and said a silent prayer the letter was long forgotten.

Later, in Miami, I learn of his untimely death and I'm ashamed over my sense of relief.

To me, loving Andy primarily meant the feeling of joy. He looked so innocent, so sweet, so in need of my emotional support. Love wasn't a subject to be analyzed or pondered over; it was simply there to be enjoyed. Whenever I took a surreptitious look at him, a wave of absolute pleasure would roll over me. His little-boy mien showed in the way he held my hand and the ease with which he spoke of his love for me, and soon I learned to speak of mine.

In my Finnish-Swedish childhood, the verb "to love" was only appropriate if used in a love relationship between two equals and even then, it wasn't used in a casual way. It took me years of Americanization to even contemplate using it with my aging father. After my mother died and he was moving towards his own passing, I wanted to tell him I loved him – in spite of the many years wasted on discord and misunderstandings. In our last telephone conversation, I searched for words.

Although "I love you" was literally translatable, word by word, into

Swedish, it wasn't used with a parent, and my father was particularly uncomfortable with emotional expression. Nevertheless, it was the best I could do.

"Yes, yes," he interrupted my haltering burbles in our native tongue. He made no effort to say something similar in return and, yet, I could sense tenderness in his voice. Abruptly, we switched subjects. We never spoke again.

Andy and I couldn't have come from more different backgrounds. And yet, the immediate sense of connectedness between us transcended our separate heritages. In my prior relationships, my Scandinavian upbringing, which sociologists have described as stubborn independence and individualism, had often been a disadvantage so I was quite surprised when I realized what seemed to me to be a strong part of the Jewish culture, the voluntary need to stay connected, was a matter of comfort and reassurance. When he took me to see Jackie Mason, I became hooked on his "he's-too-Jewish" quips. Coming from similar pain and tragedy that Finns often spoke about, Jewish humor reminded me of my own ongoing search for the irony and the absurd when feelings of alienation and isolation threatened to overwhelm me.

"I'll call you when I park the car, I'll call when I cross the street, I'll call when...," he liked to say Jackie Mason-like with the typical grin showing he wasn't serious but he knew I found this amusing.

The child in Andy loved surprises when *he* was the one providing them, but he was emphatic about not wanting them for himself. "I like to be in control," was his standard refrain. This also meant giving gifts when he felt like it, regardless of the date on a calendar. Two days before my first birthday with him, he pulled out a Tiffany bag from under his seat in the car, insisting I open it at once, while I explained about the "Rule" that says gifts may only be opened on the "real day." Like a child, he didn't believe in delayed gratification and he didn't see any reason for waiting while I pointed out the importance of remembering certain dates at the right time.

"Every day is your birthday," he pouted till I agreed that the iconic blue box with the white ribbon was there to be opened.

It wasn't long after I moved into his apartment that I noticed a new Friday routine. Not only was it the Day of Flowers when I had to clear a space for large bunches of the roses he'd bring home, but this was always followed by an impromptu speech. "Little girl," he'd begin. "You know that one day I'm going to marry you."

And it became part of our running *shtick* that he always slept closest to the door regardless of where we were, at home or with family, or in a strange hotel room.

"I'll protect the cave so I can kill anyone who wants to hurt you," he grimaced with a feigned expression of toughness. "I'll tear them apart limb-by-limb." The thought of being protected was quite comforting for me.

Sometimes, when a street vendor approached us at a red light he rolled down his window and asked for three or four bunches of flowers for "my wonderful wife," making sellers smile as if they never witnessed that kind of love before.

If I forgot there were always the toll booth operators. When I followed him in my own car they'd tell me my fee was already paid, and whenever the clerks were female they'd often add something about how special he was. "Do you know how lucky you are?" one said.

But was it really luck that made this affectionate and unusual man choose me among the many self-assured, high-achieving Jewish women who pursued him? Or was it God's hand in my life? I took to playing devotional music, and one day I broke into tears when the following words came across the airwaves: "More valuable than silver, more precious than pure gold, is your love, your eternal love."

Without me noticing it, I'd distorted the lines between God and Andy.

In two years, we were formally engaged. Even his ex-wife congratulated me, saying her former husband was a "warm and kind" man with a "great sense of humor" and "without a mean bone in his body."

His proposal had set my head spinning and my heart on fire, but I showed little reaction. A learned and habitual lack of response, ingrained from my childhood, made me reach deep down into my internal storage of acceptable behavior so I wouldn't give away how happy I was. Jews may say their *kinehora* to keep away bad luck, but they can't hold a candle to the feigned dispassion of a woman of my alienage and family characteristics. Remaining unemotional was the operating term so that nothing would go wrong with my future with Andy. Some might believe my expression was that of an inherently deceptive person, but I was simply responding like I had 25 years before in my only other similar situation. Back then, I wasn't sure either that there'd been an outright proposal by the future father of my two sons – it seemed he placidly assumed we were getting married and I was too excited over my American prince to even hear if he formally asked me – and I remained as outwardly detached then as I was now.

At a celebratory dinner with friends and my oldest son, Andy said with champagne held high, "I've found the woman of my dreams." What we didn't know was that later that evening one of the couples, who'd "only" been dating, broke up because she wanted to be married and he didn't.

Such is the desire of most women to feel connected through marriage.

Screwdrivers To The Rescue

In the beginning, Jewishness was just something abstract we rarely talked about. "It's all a bunch of nonsense," Andy said. When he shared how his father had insisted on *Yeshiva* (Jewish school for Talmudic learning) so he could learn "more self-discipline," I couldn't wait to meet this patriarch of the family. Would he be upset I wasn't Jewish? I'd heard stories about families going into mourning, sitting *Shiva*, when a son married someone of the Christian faith. I knew I couldn't face the kind of parental chill I'd endured from my mother in the last years of her life.

My first introduction to Andy's family was to his only brother, Michael. A tall, gruff man with a large and booming voice that often gave evidence of how erudite and well-read he was, he turned to me brusquely. "So, what's it you love about my brother?" he said.

Wishing for something powerfully impressive and eloquent, I couldn't do any better than stammer, "I, I just *like* him."

Seeing Michael and his wife, Bev together, I knew I was out of place. They seemed to thrive on their deafening (*are they fighting*?) opinions on everything; if it wasn't the *book-du-jour* in the *New York Times* or what the Philadelphia councilmen were or weren't doing for the city, it was Bev's commentary on the rules of Judaism, which she seemed to be pronouncing for my benefit. At first fascinated, I listened, but increasingly I found myself unable to be around her shrill voice and what seemed like constant disagreements. *Americans sure could benefit from the quiet dignity of Scandinavians.*

"Don't believe everything Bev says," Andy warned me one day with a wink.

I don't know if that's what led me to an extra degree of vigilance when his Alzheimer-ridden mother later passed away in her nineties. We were already in the apartment he owned in Philadelphia, so I immediately looked in the bedroom closet where I, too, kept some clothing. Nothing suitable for the service and interment.

"I don't have anything to wear," I said to Andy.

Dark colors hadn't been a part of my normal wardrobe since I left Finland with the dreary, bleak, somber clothing of my Nordic youth. My new life had made me revel in wearing bright colors, and it wasn't until Andy said he didn't like me in red that I started modifying. Out with most tropical hues but still, rarely any black.

"Really nothing to wear to a funeral," I repeated with a silent expectation that Andy would come to my rescue and suggest a quick trip to *Bloomies*, the paragon of cosmopolitan sophistication for me.

Instead he said, "I'll call Bev. She's your size and she has plenty of black."

The thought of asking his sister-in-law for help scared me. I was afraid of her blunt opinions – "not in the business of making friends" – and the idea of being forthcoming with my own wishes was unthinkable. In old Scandinavian tradition, my family had prided itself on quiet self-sufficiency. Not asking for favors was part of it.

"No, no, no," I pleaded without avail. He was already on the phone with Bev.

"Here, talk with her."

I sputtered, I stammered, I prattled and apologized. Didn't want to cause any problem but I'd come to the city unprepared and Andy wanted me to wear black to the funeral, and… and….

"Nonsense," Bev interrupted. "Wear what you want; this isn't a funeral where you have to wear black."

"I don't?" I was puzzled. *Not wear black to a funeral?*

In a strange sense I was relieved. My role in the family had just been confirmed. Bev wanted me to look foolish. Didn't I know it all along. Once an outsider, always an outsider. Hopefully, Andy would fix it.

I wanted to get off the phone, but Bev wasn't about to let me go yet.

"That's the Christian way," she said as if talking about some contagious condition. "Jews aren't required to wear black."

I wore black, pieced together from odd pieces I'd previously left in the Philly apartment, and so did everyone else. And yet, I couldn't stop myself from feeling different. While Ben, the head of the family, and Andy's brother with his wife formed a line in the oldest Jewish funeral home in Philadelphia, I agonized. *Should I sit, should I stand? Should I be next to Andy or try blending into the crowd in the back? I'm sure they can tell I'm a* shikse *in an unfamiliar setting.*

Unlike in the Helsinki of my youth, people I didn't know approached me with words of sympathy for my loss. When the family was finally ushered into the first row of the packed room Andy grabbed my hand and kept me close to him. Once again, he made me feel safe and protected.

Thankfully, Ben had readily embraced me when we first met. Offering me a Screwdriver, he said, "You Finns like vodka, no?" From then on, this became "our" drink, a necessary balm for my jittery nerves as I imagined him asking me about the wartime history of Finland, including the fate of the Jews, like those American tourists of his generation had done in Helsinki.

"But your life is so much more interesting," I said in a preemptive move that'd keep my future father-in-law from sharing what I believed would be his vast knowledge of Marshall Mannerheim and the Finnish Jews. Better stop him now before I ended up looking totally foolish in front of his son.

As I managed to get from Ben, his road from a small Ukrainian town with a 30% Jewish population began with the First World War when his mother hid him from the expected military conscription. Somehow, he managed to find his way to Vienna, followed by a stint as a Young Pioneer in Palestine, still under the British Mandate. Afraid of the malaria ravaging the area, he decided to return home, but during a stop-over in Marseilles he had one of those inexplicable moments of luck that saved many a doomed Jew from the Holocaust: he was offered the last ticket on a ship to America. When, in 1939, he entered into a commercial arrangement with someone he'd just met, his legacy as a successful businessman in Philadelphia was established.

"Now, about your Marshall Mannerheim…," he said, returning to the subject of the Finnish wartime hero. I held my breath. *Just let him talk.* I was always a good listener and now, feeling the soothing effects of the Screwdriver, I knew I could wait this one out to see in what direction the wiry old man was heading with the topic. No need to add anything, at least not now.

Slightly shifting to another historical track, he said, "Hitler really respected Finland…, I remember reading about his visit to Helsinki, and then Himmler's, but we really didn't learn much about how the Jews survived in your country?"

Although there was a definite question mark at the end of his sentence, I said nothing. I sipped my Screwdriver, grateful that Ben continued reminiscing without any assistance by me.

During our next visit, Ben waved at me a thin segment of a book he obviously finished already. Quite a voracious reader, he had a habit that greatly disturbed Andy: he tore books into sections before reading them and then he threw away each part as he moved through the pages. This wasn't as annoying as it was unsettling to Andy, who increasingly seemed to be craving order and exactness in all aspects of his life. When his father said to me, "I saved this part for you," Andy's distress was clear. "What did you do with the rest of it?" he demanded of his father, who just shook his head as if he didn't understand his son. Without a word, Ben then handed me what he'd saved for me.

With a quick glance through the pages I saw the word "Finland" flickering by, but wait, *what was this about deportations*? As far as I knew, my homeland took great pride in the fact that none of its Jews had been deported. My father even told me about the Jewish-Finnish war veterans and, together, we'd visited the special part of a cemetery set aside for them. Surely, there was a mistake in Ben's book. Vaguely, I said to him we'd talk more about this during our next visit. As if I even had an idea what the "more" meant. By this time, the calming effect of the Screwdriver was sweeping over me; my anxiety over appearing stupid or just generally uninformed was about to dissipate.

Today, I regret no longer being able to share with Ben the stories I now know. Born in 1899, he'd hoped to live to 100 so he could say he lived in three centuries, but he missed the target with a few months. Given a second chance, I'd want to make absolutely sure he knew of the brave Jewish soldiers in the Finnish army who fought along Nazi soldiers from Germany to save Finland from total annihilation by Soviet forces. These heroes deserve a special chapter.

Co-Belligerents And The *Schul*

When Isak Smolar, a Finnish citizen and a Jew, got the notice from his draft board there was never any question he wouldn't defend his home country when it was invaded by the Soviet Union in November 1939. This so-called Winter War was followed by a second war when Hitler attacked the Soviet Union in 1941 and Finland decided to join with him against the common enemy. Both countries had a different reason for their actions: Hitler with his quest for *Lebensraum* and world dominance, and Finland with its need for survival as a nation.

This joining of forces resulted in Wehrmacht and SS troops fighting side-by-side with not only Finnish but Jewish-Finnish soldiers, like Isak Smolar (for a total of 350 Jews in the two wars). Without a written agreement, the two countries were *co-belligerents* fighting the same cause. More importantly, at no time was Finland occupied by or a formal ally of Hitler. As my father, a war veteran himself, pointed out, "co-belligerence" may not matter to others, but it does to a Finn.

The son of a rabbi, Isak was known as Sholka, in the typical Finnish fashion of having a moniker of some sort, regardless of how short a real first or last name seems to be (what could possibly be so hard about either Isak or Smolar?).

Nicknamed after his older brother, Solomon, who was also called Sholka, Isak became "Little Sholka" and eventually just Sholka when the brother emigrated to Israel. Today, this is the name that's inextricably linked to the tent-like structure called Sholka's *Schul* on the Russian front.

Although many other religions were practiced in Finland, and Judaism was a small but protected part of them, no religious provisions had been made for Jews in the Finnish army. Since the country Sholka was fighting for had two officially recognized state churches (Lutheran and Greek Orthodox) it's no surprise that the Christian conscripts already had their clergy at the front (my father was one of them) who led them in prayers and ministered to the wounded and dying.

In the trenches, Sholka contemplated all this and decided to take action. What he wanted was a place to worship, not just the time to do so. The unusual request by this Jewish draftee, who rose to the rank of corporal, went straight to the top of the army brass.

Not only was he given a large white canvas tent (some describe it as being made of plywood or millboard) like officers used, but he also had six men at his disposal for the project. Some sources say there were even German soldiers among his helpers. A pipe stove kept the place warm for the weekly Saturday services, and windows let the natural light in. The Helsinki congregation donated the Torah scroll.

"We notified all soldiers of the Mosaic faith," Sholka wrote later. "And we explained that they'd get the necessary leave to participate in services." He, himself, made sure to go there every Friday to make sure everything was in order for the upcoming Shabbat.

Soon, the place was filled. There were Jewish soldiers, who, as Sholka pointed out, had never been seen at services back home. And then there were the Finnish Gentiles and German Nazis, who often skied or rode their horses for miles just to check out the unusual house of worship. Long after the war, snippets appeared about the Jewish soldiers explaining their faith to the curious visitors, German Nazis and Christians alike, and how there were no confrontations between the two camps. Nor were there instances of Nazis refusing to salute or cooperate with Jewish-Finnish officers. In fact, the attitude of the Germans is described as one of genuine curiosity and even admiration. If one of them asked a Finn about the Jewish situation in Finland the usual answer was, "There's no difference between Jews and other soldiers in the Finnish Army."

Some Germans said they never met a Jew before and some hadn't seen a synagogue either, although this tent-like structure where services were held hardly met their expectations.

Over the years, and as memories have a tendency to color recollections, the place has alternatively been known as *Sholka's Shul*, or the *Portable, Tent*, or *Field Synagogue*. Because of its location by the Svir River in an Eastern province of Finland, it also came to be known as the *Svir Prayer Tent*, or just the *Prayer Tent*. I guess it depends on who's doing the telling.

There's no evidence of what name Sholka would have preferred for his creation. All we know is the pride he felt and that he worried about the structure. He says in his papers that he didn't want to draw any attention to it so when one day he found a window and one of the pipes to the heater missing, he decided not to report the incident. A few days later he was called in to see the captain of his battalion and although he couldn't recall having done anything against regulations, he was afraid he was going to be reprimanded for something unknown. Why else would he be called for?

"Is it true that things have been stolen from your synagogue?" the captain demanded.

"Yes, Sir."

At that, the head of the battalion slammed his fist on the table and bellowed, "That's desecration of a *church*!"

Sholka took this expression of anger as proof of how protective Finnish officers were towards the Jews.

Whatever the unusual place of worship did to enlighten the German Nazis who fought for Finland, nothing prepared them for the lack of respect their

Jewish-Finnish brothers-in-arms showed for the Iron Cross, the distinctive medal first commissioned by the Kaiser in 1813 and later appropriated by Hitler. When I went searching for stories about this military decoration to share during my lectures, I found the following about the Nazi decoration given to some Finnish Jews:

First, there's Salomon Klass, the rare Jewish citizen of Finland who had attended the Reserve Officers' School, while most of his comrades were enlisted men. Captain Klass was also an avowed Zionist who moved to Palestine four years before the Winter War broke out in 1939. When he got the Finnish draft notice he returned home, where he was promptly put in charge of blowing up a strategic bridge. After another successful battle he lost one eye to a Russian bullet, but still went on to fight in the so-called Continuation War, where word about his valor travelled fast to his superiors. A Finnish General is said to have introduced him to German officers as "one of my best company commanders," knowing very well Klass was Jewish.

One day, a Nazi officer made a special visit to personally thank him for saving the lives of many German soldiers. That's when he noticed Klass had an accent when they conversed in German. Perhaps he was from another Baltic country?

"You may be hearing my native tongue, which is Yiddish," the captain said. "You see, I'm a Jew and my parents came from the Baltics."

There was a moment of awkward silence. Then, the German Nazi shook the hand of this Jewish Finn once again. "I personally have nothing against you as a Jew," he said. As he turned to leave, he raised his arm in the Nazi salute and called out Heil Hitler for everyone to hear.

Later, Klass was told he'd shown disrespect towards a superior officer but the Germans still wanted to honor him with the Iron Cross. There's no record of what reason he gave for turning it down, but, on the other hand, nothing else may be needed.

Then there's Leo Skurnick, a Jewish-Finnish medical major, who referred to the Hippocratic oath when fellow soldiers asked why he bothered to give aid to

German soldiers, often even performing surgery on them. Since the Nazi habit was to abandon their wounded on the battle fields, Skurnick soon became known for dragging them into the field hospital, where he cared for Finnish and German soldiers alike. It's said he saved over 600 members of the SS in one fight alone.

One Finnish colonel is on record with saying about Major Skurnick, "He didn't only take care of the wounded; he also went to the frontline to bring them back under enemy fire. Regardless of whether they were Finns or Germans, he brought them to safety."

Skurnick also expressed compassion for the young boys from Berlin who, towards the end of the war, had been sent to the Finnish territory for the fight against the Soviets. Most of this crop of German soldiers were high-school and university students who were afraid to go into the darkness of the woods where they knew Russians were waiting to brutally slaughter any enemy within their reach.

When the major learned he was up for an Iron Cross he passed word to the Germans that they "can wipe their *arses* with it." Some stories have the Nazis demanding revenge for his impertinence, but others have a Finnish General saving Skurnick's hide.

The third, Jewish-Finnish awardee of the Iron Cross was a female nurse, Dina Poljakoff, who served in a military hospital where it fell on her to care for Germans injured in a torpedo attack outside Helsinki. When she received the invitation to the awards ceremony, she surprised her family by saying she'd go to the appointed place.

With a straight back and head held high, she walked up to the table where the ribboned medals were laid out. After looking them over, she turned on her heels and walked out without saying a word.

To this group of brave Finns who rejected a Nazi decoration is sometimes added another person deserving a special mention: one Jewish Lieutenant, Leo Jakobson, assigned to military headquarters as a German translator when he happened across the names of all awardees-to-be. Seeing his name on the list, he quietly removed it without telling anyone.

There are no reports of any later repercussions from these refusals of the Iron Cross. It seems at first the stories simply disappeared into history as another peculiarity with the Finnish situation. The international press much preferred to write about the Finnish Jews and the German Nazis fighting as fellow combatants in the theatre of war. It was those stories that made headlines around the world, even reaching Jerusalem where a 1947 convention of Jewish war veterans denounced their Finnish coreligionists for "having been on the side of the Nazis."

When I share these wartime stories during my presentations, there's usually someone who's incredulous. Can it really be true that these Jewish Finns had the courage to challenge the Nazis in this manner? Why is it that the Holocaust-related literature rarely includes stories like these?

I have no answer. But I have a theory. The culture of Finland (indeed, all of Scandinavia, as I said in my previous mentions of the ancient code of conduct called *Jante's Law* – although perhaps modified by each succeeding generation) still disapproves of people who're overt achievers and, worse, have the audacity to be proud of it. Or, as my mother said when I mistakenly wrote to her about a commendation I'd received for my work in Miami, *Don't think that makes you special*. No wonder, I think, that you have to dig deep to learn about all the *Sholkas* in wartime Finland.

Guns And The Ghost

Back in my former country my mother was dying, and I couldn't stomach the thought of going to her deathbed. I cried over having to face her because I believed our estrangement had made me weaker. Andy held me while I exhausted myself with tears and then he took control.

"You'll always regret it if you don't go now," he said. "Take one of your sons with you, since I have to be at the office."

Even with one of them as a travel companion, I didn't want to go. The only one who understood this was a Swedish friend in Miami. We agreed that "nobody in America," particularly one with Jewish values, understood family rejection as we did. We alone had a lock on self-pity and exclusion.

But when Andy added, "If you don't go, it may affect our relationship" I was convinced. He got the plane tickets and booked a hotel. My brother said they never knew anyone with so much kindness and wisdom that he'd send his fiancée and her son to the funeral of an impending mother-in-law he'd never get to meet. My sister was unimpressed and aloof, hovering over our father like a surrogate wife.

Andy's parting words for me were to tell my father that we'd soon be visiting him. "Ask him for the name of his favorite bottle of booze," he said.

But I never got close enough to ask. My sister guarded his space as if expecting me to say something so inappropriate – and liquor was a large part of what was her *verboten* – that I'd cause our father to drop dead from the sheer shock of it. When he looked at me with glaucoma-clouded eyes, I thought I saw a trace of the old days when he alone could find something humorous or positive in any given situation. I wanted him to tell me that with mother gone we'd get right back to times of laughter and innocence.

When I returned home it was as if I had a new awareness of my relationship with Andy. In the throes of romantic love I'd only seen sweet little oddities that came with the man who had swept me off my feet. Now, when I looked around his apartment I only saw a bachelor pad filled with hundreds of books, neatly piled high in all corners of his place and double- and triple-lined onto drooping shelves. But I loved to read, too. Besides, it made the apartment look homey as if he were an early promoter of *hygge*, the Scandinavian concept for all things cozy spreading throughout the US many years later. So what that he had an anger attack when something wasn't in the exact place he expected? He was a long-time bachelor who liked order in his life. And wasn't it just so *endearing* when the precisely stacked rows of newspapers, and magazines, and rubber-banded mail grew to man-sized heights that looked like they'd topple over at a moment's notice? Even when he was perpetually *getting ready* to pay routine household bills, I said to myself this was merely a very conscientious and organized man.

Meanwhile, his concern for my physical welfare remained a constant. Eating out or going to the movies automatically prompted him to remind me to take along a sweater and if I happened to forget, there were two spares in the trunk of his car which was also loaded with maps, flashlights and ropes, Miami phonebooks, pens and paper, raingear and hats, all neatly packed into two plastic snap-lock containers. Two extra sweaters lay meticulously folded in their own cloth bag.

Whenever he pulled into the parking garage of his building he opened the trunk seemingly to make sure things hadn't shifted around, which they never had, so that he could take a surreptitious inventory of his belongings. At first, I merely observed, thinking how much self-discipline he had, compared to the rest of us who merely throw things in the trunk and certainly never check it each time we reach home.

But one day, curiosity finally got to me or maybe it was a sudden bout of impatience as I once again stood waiting for him to finish the trunk routine. Exasperated, I said: "Why do you do that? Can't we go upstairs to the apartment *once* without opening the trunk?"

"What do you mean?" His sheepish smile was a dead give-away that he knew exactly what I was referring to.

"All this unnecessary stuff you have to do while I wait and wait and wait…, I'm really amazing myself that I have patience for all this," I challenged.

"Oh, *that*." He was nonplused as if we were talking about the weather. But after a brief pause, while the twinkle reached for the corner of his deep-blue eyes, he said, "And you think life with *you* is easy!"

Although he was a master at deflecting my annoyance with his play-like way of turning a difficult situation into a humorous comment like that, the scene planted a seed in me. *Rituals*, I thought then, fearing that these were a sign of something I couldn't quite pinpoint. As usual, I turned to my journal where I admonished myself to "remember that there's a season for the soul too – not only the soil – and I must hold on to that thought." The self-indulgent entry, going on for four pages of tightly, hand-written words, also said, "Even if I never saw him again, I'll never forget how he stirred something in me that I never felt before. As if I finally *belong*. If I were into New Age and Shirley MacLaine, I'd probably describe it as a past-life experience."

In these private writings I continued to push aside the notion that the rituals and other frequently odd actions could be something more than a slight peculiarity with the man I loved.

Till the thing with his gun collection hit me. Or, more correctly, what one of his friends said one day.

"Real Jews don't have guns."

Andy became predictably angry because he loved his amassment of guns for what they ultimately were: possessions to be sorted, organized, and controlled at his discretion. Asking him to get rid of them because he was Jewish would be like telling a child he could no longer have any toys because of the color of his hair.

He didn't own just a few weapons, but he had a veritable stockpile, most of which was in a large locked safe, made from solid steel and bolted to the concrete floor of the apartment. Only he had the key to this arsenal. He also hid small handguns in different bags and containers, and he kept a loaded pistol in the glove compartment of the car as well as another one in the drawer next to his bed.

When I spoke of my overall fear of weapons, and particularly loaded ones, he said an unloaded gun was useless. Then, he bought me a *Sig Sauer* pistol and insisted I join him in the practice range one Saturday morning. The whole scene frightened me, and, after that, I didn't pick up a gun again.

"How are you going to protect yourself?" Andy said, annoyed at me not going along in this activity. When I said I didn't understand what I needed to be protected against, he spoke vaguely about how Jews in America could be at risk of persecution like their European comrades during the Holocaust. "If the Jews had been armed during the war, they could have beaten the Nazis." When I mumbled about different times and this being the United States, he said only another hunter would understand. This made even less sense to me, but I said nothing more.

One day he asked me to go with him to a hunting lodge in South Carolina. "But don't tell my friends," he said in a tone that had a real sharpness to it.

"Why not?" I asked, puzzled that something like that should be kept secret.

"You wouldn't understand, but it's Yom Kippur and I don't want them to know we're hunting on a holiday."

"Maybe we shouldn't go, then?"

"There you go again, not knowing anything about Judaism. Of course, we're going."

When we arrived, his fellow hunters (all Latin Catholics) from his home shooting range in Miami were in the middle of preparing for the following day's event but Andy wanted to go shopping. Although the back of his specially-equipped SUV already brimmed with hunting paraphernalia we made two trips to stores where he spent three hours selecting more camouflage clothing with matching bags, scentless soaps, rifle scopes, and, the ultimate bliss, a seat that could be hoisted high up in the trees. Before the sun rose the next morning and he left, he was primed with gear that would have done any deerstalker proud.

Later, with the traditional blood-mark on his forehead, he cheerfully posed for pictures next to his stag, before arranging for the carcass to be cut up and frozen in individual portions of meat to be shipped back home. It wasn't until Andy was out of earshot that the organizer of the day's expedition told everyone that he, the leader, had had to shoot the injured animal. In spite of what he told friends at home; Andy never killed that deer.

After this, we went on many other "hunting" trips but, once we got there, he usually pled fatigue. Instead, and with everyone else gone for the day, we scouted local stores for still more guns, ammunition and clothing. The process was always frantic and endless, followed by hours of repetitive sorting and organizing that seemed to calm him. Each time his actions brought back memories of a moving picture that followed me wherever we travelled: Andy, at home, with a jagged *Gerber* fishing knife that looked like a dagger.

I didn't want to see this reel again, but one scene still kept repeating itself in an irritatingly cinematic fashion: Trancelike, he was stroking the sharp blade over and over again, sometimes while watching TV and at other times sitting on the edge of his bed. He was in a world of his own and I couldn't tell if he was soothed by the rhythmic motion or if this was one of those actions ruled by some invisible force. Was there a secret code that only he knew? Could it be – *no, I must push those thoughts aside*! – that there was something else going on with him?

Ostensibly because I had started having crying jags in the most unanticipated situations, I secretly made an appointment with a therapist, a Jewish psychiatrist from Venezuela by way of California.

It wasn't long before he was asking questions about my relationship. Because I learned as a child not to talk, good or bad, about immediate family, it was at first impossible to be critical. I used the defensive tactics of a psychologically battered woman and said feeble things about how I just couldn't please my man who was the nicest, the best, and the most loving and caring.

"I don't understand why life is so difficult for my fiancée...," I finally ventured in the faltering voice of my own insecurities.

"Agony and angst are part of who we are as Jews," the therapist said. I dutifully recorded his words in my journal, as if the words themselves would provide relief.

In the next session I tried sharing my agony over Andy's "problems." When the analyst suggested I let life evolve on its own, without worrying so much, I had a temporary sense of peace. After all, this was a professional therapist urging me to "go with the flow." For a few weeks, life actually became easier. But then something happened, something that I later pointed to as Jungian synchronicity.

It was after a particularly difficult day and I'd just settled into the bedroom to read after my customary post-dinner clean-up when I heard the loud clink of things being shuffled around in the dishwasher. Cautiously tiptoeing to the kitchen, I found him in a frenzy re-organizing everything I had already done. Big plates had to be with big plates, followed by small with small and, similarly on the top-rack, glasses had to be in exact rows by decreasing sizes. Naturally, the silverware had to be separated by individual function.

"Can't you do anything right?" His voice was frantic but not quite at the point of full-blown anger, although I sensed a build-up. "You even left bits of food on here!"

"Isn't that what a dishwasher is for? It'll wash off the remains," I said.

"That doesn't make it right and you should know it." The tension in his voice increased.

In an instant, I felt the familiar knot in my stomach, reminding me of my mother's life-long criticism. That night I went to bed silently crying over my failure as a partner for the man I loved. During that sleepless night, deeply buried thoughts fought for my attention till one of them could no longer be kept away: the crazy, hidden force that made him go through a set of motions till he was satisfied. I'd read about rituals and uncontrollable compulsions – even Howard Hughes paraded through the recesses of my mind – and I thought *maybe, just maybe, Andy was obsessive-compulsive*. Sure, all of us throw labels around for various and sundry reasons but in the darkness of my misery this suddenly resonated with me.

During my next session with the therapist I asked for his opinion. "Is it possible that Andy is an obsessive-compulsive?"

"But he works?" He stated what he already knew from previous sessions, with only a tinge of questioning in his tone.

"Of course; he goes to the office every day."

"And he makes a good living?"

"Yes, I'd say so." Andy said so himself, so I guessed that qualified.

"You go out with friends and you travel; right?"

"Yes, but he takes forever to get ready and we're never on time because of all his rituals. And you know about his collections of *things*."

"But his unusual habits don't interfere to the extent that he can't function and therefore he's not obsessive-compulsive. You can't be a little bit; you either are or you aren't, and he isn't."

That session put a temporary end to my feeble attempt to find a name for the banshee that kept interfering with our lives and had brought on my deep sadness. I felt foolish over having tried an absentee diagnosis and I chided myself for being too critical and demanding.

It took me several months to re-consider the diagnosis, or rather lack thereof, but the seeds were planted. His fixations became increasingly more unpredictable and inconsistent and just when I thought I had gotten used to one, another would crop up. I was never on the right page and never could fully anticipate an outburst or a certain action, regardless of how I tried being more observant. I was constantly on edge, watching him flee into his own frenzy of sorting or organizing something as if he were about to lose control. Still, I kept hoping that my love for him would calm him.

"Hope is the only thing I truly own now," I recorded in my journal that was now filling with overall ruminations on hope and other existential questions. Somewhere I read that miracles often happen to those who, through despair, can feel optimism so I was determined to do whatever I could on my own to nurture the hope that, somehow, I was going to understand what was "wrong" with Andy so that it could be "fixed." Self-delusion is a powerful tool.

It was a miracle he could control himself in public. Outsiders didn't suspect anything and continued to speak of his sweet persona, which was quite evident to all. Nobody knew of his secret behavior and I believe friends would have been horrified if they suspected it. Even when it caused me fear and agony, I didn't speak about it. I just kept vacillating between my roles as the self-proclaimed Silent Caregiver – or was it the Big Enabler? – and the overtly upbeat medical-slash-mental sleuth as I stubbornly held on to the thought that there simply must be a name, a diagnosis, for what ailed him. "If only he'd get counseling," I journaled. And the enabler in me wrote: "I'll go along to show that I can learn to deal with it."

All I wanted was an official name for his strange behavior, something that could make me understand that third person in our relationship, that ghost which nobody could control. I wanted to understand it – befriend it – so that it'd lose its powers over us.

I dropped hints to his daughter, a social worker who often spoke of dealing with mental health issues of her clients. After one of our visits to see her, she spent an inordinate amount of private time with her father. Afterwards, she took me aside and said wistfully, "I think you'll now get him to go to counseling with you." Why was I instantly filled with guilt, as if I were incapable of making her father happy and whole?

Four months later, after two difficult weeks of particularly mad behavior, we were spending a leisurely day at the beach when Andy suddenly turned to me with that little-boy smile that made him look as if he'd been caught in some mischief. "I've been to a therapist," he said. "She wants you to come with me to the next appointment."

And so it came to be that, almost three years into our relationship, something was set in motion that made Andy admit he was often besieged by an un-named monster. After just a few sessions, we got a name for this curious mental condition. He suffered, we were told, from an "Obsessive-Compulsive Disorder" and that made him a card-carrying "OCDer." The condition was controllable by medication and behavioral modification.

So, there *was* a name for whatever made him act so strangely and it wasn't my fault, after all. Andy himself was both comforted and concerned. The idea that there was a scientific term for his impulses gave him visible relief, but he balked at the advice that he should be on prescription drugs and also see a behavioral therapist on a long-term basis. "I'm not taking any more meds than I already am," he said while I bit my tongue. As a person who stays away from chemical additions to my daily life, I could relate to his feelings but, at the same time, I was elated over the diagnosis. "We have a name, we have a name," I kept repeating to myself as I got lost in the illusion that an official identification of his mental illness would somehow ease the burden of dealing with it. Hope does strange things.

Leaving the therapist's office on that balmy August day that's forever etched in my mind, we hugged each other in the parking lot. "Will you still love me?" he asked with an impish smile that melted any steely resolve I had for just a fleeting second to insist on him seeing an OCD-expert. "You know I'll always love you," I assured him. My poor Andy *needed* me and, more than that, he only wanted to be loved for who he was.

As we stood there holding each other, my nostrils delighted in the aroma of him, whom I loved so deeply, and I felt as if my heart was going to burst. My love would turn him into St. George, who'd slay the OCD-dragon all by himself. My devotion would give him strength to do anything. So I thought.

And God Laughed

I wish I could say life became smoother for Andy after the diagnosis, but instead, his odd actions increased in frequency, probably because he wasn't ready to admit to the severity of his mental disorder. If anything, our sessions with the therapist stirred up additional conflicts in his sub-conscious. He was referring to his condition as "it," in a tone of voice of a child imitating a grown-up, but it always seemed as if he were talking about something not even remotely concerning him. I don't think he ever believed the diagnosis – and who actually knows if it was correct, since mental health experts can't agree on what exactly constitutes OCD – because of his innate tendency towards distrust of the world.

Meanwhile, I learned from the literature that OCDers could be classified as *hoarders, counters, orderers,* and *checkers*, and the difference between "normal behavior" – if there's such a thing – and OCD-induced actions is the amount of time and energy spent on the intrusive patterns. With Andy, this included the lack of any concept of time when he was drawn into one of his bouts of uncontrollable behavior. Because of the rituals that had to be performed regardless of the day's schedule or other plans, time was his biggest enemy. Hairbrushes had to be cleaned, shavers diligently blown dry, and solid wastes had to be checked for blood with a large flashlight before they were flushed down the toilet. But when he walked out of his bathroom all I saw was a man who'd just left his things perfectly organized and needed me to make the rest of his day as routine as possible. Both gullible and perceptive, vulnerable and strong, helpless and in control, he was a child and a real man. There was simply no pretense or guile about him; he was who he was.

My reading also told me that paranoia, anxiety and depression frequently go hand-in-hand with OCD, like they did with him, but these could also be separate disorders. Somewhere I even read when an affluent person suffers from OCD we tend to call him "eccentric" – and get away with it – whereas a poor person is quickly labeled "crazy" and socially shunned.

For a person with Andy's kind of OCD, books had long ago taken on a life of their own. It was clear he loved his ever-growing print collection for what it ultimately was, another belonging that could be controlled and put into something resembling an order. They were also the reason for why we almost didn't move from his bachelor apartment into the beautiful condo he'd bought and re-furbished to his exact specifications. "This is for when we get married," he said in a calm moment. And I'd immediately slip into my romantic fantasy of creating a peaceful, happy life with him.

Most people I knew hired professionals for their Moving Day, and that was it. Not us. Since we weren't going to keep any of the furniture from his old place, and we were moving to a lot of built-ins, it was a matter of transferring only personal stuff. We did it carload by carload, with the exception of his overwhelming book collection, which demanded an extra-special process. I knew it'd take some creativity and a bit of conspiracy by me, because nobody was a bigger expert than Andy on turning the simplest task into a major-league event.

Fortunately, illness intervened; not his, but mine.

We'd planned to fly north to visit his brother when I got the flu. I remained in the old place while Andy reluctantly made the trip alone. Before he left, he gave permission for me to pack the books and take them to our new home, although at the time I was asking him I couldn't see myself even getting out of bed. My head was spinning, my body ached, and my throat was on fire. But I'd made up my mind; the books must be taken to our new home before his return or we'd never move. And a no-move meant no wedding.

"Keep an eye on them at all times," he said as I dropped him off at the airport. "Never leave them alone. You don't know who'll want to steal them."

I remember this period vividly because I still owe Matt Drudge and Michael Isikoff. As their press reports on Monica Lewinsky broke into the national news my brain got just enough stimulation, without requiring any thinking at all, for me to survive the menial work of stuffing an endless amount of books into manageable cardboard boxes.

The sneezing, coughing and sniffling lulled me into believing that he'd be thrilled with the result: after all, he didn't have to do the *schlepping*. In my feverish mind, I could already hear one of his favorite expressions: "There are work horses and then there are show horses," which was usually a part of his running *shtick* about his own insistence that only he could do something the right way.

On the way home from the airport, I prepared him.

"Wait till you see my surprise. I really did something terrific."

To play the sympathy card, I added a few words about how very, very sick I'd been but in spite of that I'd become a workhorse, just like he'd said I could. By the time we got to the front door of what was soon to be his former bachelor pad he was curious like a child. He closed his eyes as I helped him step inside.

"Now, open your eyes!" I squeezed his arm with anticipated pleasure.

Instead, his mouth dropped at the sight of the dark hollows of the cleaned-out bookcases. Sweat began dripping from his forehead. He grabbed my hand and put it on his heart: it was beating a mile a minute. My poor sweetheart was having an anxiety attack! And then the OCD raised its annoying head even more as it demanded that I recount a step-by-step description of how I'd packed the books, sealed the boxes with extra-strong packing tape, marked them with black markers exactly the way he wanted, carried them downstairs to the garage, loaded them on the hired hand's pick-up where I never left them unattended, moved them over, and reversed the process at our new place.

His question "where's the inventory list?" finally put me over the edge. I laughed till my sides hurt and tears were falling. Although he finally joined me, it'd take close to an hour before he stopped talking about the "how" and "when" of my work. After that, he never spoke of it again.

Often I thought about where to draw the line between his need to control his environment and obvious bullying, and although I kept mum on those feelings I tried setting minor boundaries, one of which involved the Miami *Herald*. For years he subscribed to three daily papers which kept piling up, unread, in his apartment. My habit, on the other hand, was to start each day with the local news, but regardless of how careful I was with folding the pages back in their original order it wasn't good enough. One day when he was particularly down, he ordered me to, "Get your own subscription. I don't want a paper that someone else has already read."

"But you never look at it!" I countered in a flash of assertiveness mixed with a dose of the basic precepts of logic. "And I'm not just 'somebody' because you keep telling me I'm your wife so, unless you want me to *iron* the paper when I'm done, I'll continue reading it." Surprisingly, this was the end of that dilemma.

In retrospect it seems nearly impossible to believe it only took one year for the renovation of our new apartment, the place that I could finally call home. Or could I? You didn't have to be a psychologist to see the significance of the floorplan although, ironically, I was responsible for that myself. In preparation for the new design, Andy had hired an architect who proposed four different lay-outs, all of which made me spend hours thinking of ways to re-configure the space. In the middle of one sleepless night I grabbed a piece of paper and started drafting. I gave myself a small interior, window-less office next to my own bathroom and closet, only fleetingly thinking that others might look at the space as "housekeeper's quarters." For him, I sketched a large office by one of the beautiful balconies, and an enormous walk-in closet at the opposite end of what was a peculiarly long unit; in actuality, two apartments joined by the previous owners, who'd carved out small rabbit-hole type bedrooms for their four children. Expecting the usual put-down, I could barely believe it when he gave my drawings to the architect to put in workable order. I always knew I had good spatial vision.

Although Andy prohibited me ("you know I like my privacy") from inviting any of my friends to see our new place, he liked nothing more than showing it to his, one of whom commented on the placement and smallness of my space, "You can really tell who rules this place." Others focused on his closets, normally locked to everyone including me, but which he liked to show off during this reveal. What he didn't seem to realize was that the scrupulously arranged order of his clothes and other belongings hinted, at least to most viewers, at something peculiar about their friend.

Meanwhile, our wedding plans had been going nowhere, as the inevitable practicalities seemed insurmountable. First, there was the matter of accommodating the schedule of his family, and then there was the hurdle of furnishing a large apartment. When those two factors were no longer relevant the matter of where to have the wedding ceremony and festivities cropped up. He didn't want to be the "center of attention" so the event had to be small. Ben suggested his country club and Bev offered to host it at her weekend home in the Pennsylvania hills. But Andy objected to each; it either wasn't personal enough or he didn't want "us" to relinquish control to his sister-in-law. The obstacles were endless. Once one was cleared another one inevitably appeared. Now there was "paperwork to be done" and that required time he didn't have. And, what to do about a rabbi?

Although Andy was a self-proclaimed non-believer, he wanted a religious service. A few calls connected me to rabbis willing to perform a wedding between two gays but not a Gentile and a Jew, so that was yet another bump on the road to our wedding. Ben said his rabbinical friend in Israel would come to the States to perform the ceremony but first I had to convert. Before I could contemplate what I thought was a life-altering action (*how could I deny my own religious roots?*), Andy said, "Forget about conversion."

Andy had long used a Yiddish expression, *Mann tracht und Gott lacht*, often quoted by Woody Allen as, "If you want to make God laugh, tell him about your plans." When he was in a relatively calm, non-OCD mood and was able to face the inevitable changes and temporary bumps on the road of life, he'd shrug and say, "Er lacht" as if he were someone who liked going with the flow of life. But if he was in an OCD-induced moment of paranoia – another unsettling aspect of his mental condition – he fell right back into the old accusatory behavior when he shouted about all the things that were wrong with the world. Thievery was one of them.

With what now seems like great regularity but which probably occurred without any pattern at all, he was convinced "someone" had absconded with a particular pair of pants or socks, or a specific shirt still with the price tag on it; all from his locked closet to which only he kept a hidden key. Each time I told myself it was only a temporary incident. His unswerving eye for details and his obsession with things being "just right" added to my feelings of being all the more protected from harm, so maybe I was imagining something or exaggerating the situation. To make him laugh over the suspected thefts, really to break the tension, I'd then break into the Swedish *oj, oj, oj* (each pronounced "oy") but he only responded with his insistence that this was a Yiddish expression reserved for Jews. And later again, out of the blue, something would trigger the invisible force that made him unable to control his impulses to engage in irrational activities.

None of that came to matter when God finally laughed at the absurdity of our life.

One beautiful April evening, three years after the OCD diagnosis, Andy suddenly stopped talking. Soundlessly moving his lips, he tried in vain to say something while I, disobeying his suddenly vehement shout of "no, no!" called for emergency medical assistance. In less than an hour, he lay comatose on a gurney in an ambulance blaring its sirens and flashing emergency lights on the way to the hospital. *Glioblastoma, Stage IV*, an aggressive cancer in its deadliest form and without any apparent cause, had settled into the left side of his brain.

After surgery to remove the only part of the tumor that could safely be excised, the surgeon said to him, "Just go and enjoy yourself. Take up parachuting if that's what you always wanted." To us, the doctor said privately,

"Six months at the most."

And, with that my life entered another phase.

Part 3
Food And The Spirit

In the beginning of our relationship, food hadn't been something we talked much about, although when he was particularly down on himself he wanted me to serve dinners "like mother did." This meant either a three-course meal, replete with a big dessert, or lots of warm bread with butter, while he complained he was gaining too much weight.

"You're making me too fat," he'd say in the manner of a person unable to assume any responsibility for his own choices. At that time, food was another symbol for the unwanted and still un-named intrusions in his life.

Now at the end of his life, not unsurprisingly, mealtimes became a regular trigger for his anger.

"Look at this! Don't you know how to cut an orange?" With an angry motion he pointed at his plate. Grabbing a fresh fruit he'd then demonstrate how to cut it into perfectly symmetrical sections so that each wedge, when sitting by itself, faced towards the ceiling rather than slightly wobbling on one side. To me, an orange was meant to be eaten regardless of how it was cut. Still, I promised to try my best.

But the Battle of the Strawberries would go on as long as he could speak. If I sliced them, he swore he told me he only liked them whole and if I served them whole, he said I should know they were too big to eat that way. At first, I tried calming him.

"Don't you remember, Honey, that you always ate the berries whole because you said cutting them up would drain the juices?" I said.

"Nonsense, I don't know what's happening to you. Either you don't listen to what I say, or you forget."

I knew of the emotional stages of a dying person, and with Andy's already prevalent OCD-related anger issues, I expected his irrational behavior to continue. For me, little glimpses of his sweet, little-boy demeanor that had been so irresistible when we first became a couple, provided both comfort and enjoyment. One day, I watched him sitting cross-legged on the bedroom floor counting and sorting a large pile of nuts and bolts he'd retrieved from one of the many plastic containers in his closet. Tongue sticking out from one side of the mouth, he was so engrossed in the activity that he didn't even notice when I leaned over to give him a kiss on the head.

And I thought of how he used to make us stop in the middle of Philadelphia so he could peek through building barriers or push an obstacle aside to get just the right gawking angle over a construction site. At a moment like that, nothing disturbed him. I wasn't sure if he even knew he was holding on to my hand. Once, only the sound of a kneeling bus had managed to break his focus.

Turning to watch a severely deformed man maneuver his wheel-chair on the side-walk, he almost shouted at me, "Take a look at that, will you. The way he turns the wheels in all directions, and the way the bus lowers itself ..., will you just look at that!" He made no effort to lower his voice or to avert his eyes.

"Come on, come on," I'd urged under my breath. "It's humiliating and insulting for that poor man to have you stare at him like that."

"I'm not looking at him, just the wheel-chair," he shouted, totally captivated by the scene till the man was on the bus and it turned the corner.

"If I had to live like that, I'd kill myself," he said. "Nobody should live like that."

Those words now frightened me as his life was on its irreversible march toward the end. My thoughts wandered to a night out with friends, all of them Jewish, when he told everyone that disabled fetuses should be aborted. Although this led to an academic discussion about the history of eugenics and its place in the Nazi persecution of Jews he was unwilling, or unable, to see the logic in anybody else's argument.

Finally, one of his friends said, "But aren't you, as a Jew, sensitive to government-ordered abortions based on the state's idea of imperfection? If you look in your collection of Holocaust books …."

I didn't hear his answer because I rushed to the bathroom to cry. One of the other ladies came to check on me. "Don't worry, we all know how Andy is," she said in a soothing voice. When I returned to the table everyone had moved on to another subject.

Before I became an end-of-life caregiver I thought someone in my situation would immediately seek spiritual guidance. It seems when life is going well, we don't search for a higher being, call it God if you will, as much as when bad things happen and we immediately go running to our place of worship, or perhaps intensify our personal prayers. Maybe because I'd always prayed silently in bed by myself and I was turned off by organized religion, the reticent Scandinavian in me didn't consider reaching out spiritually when we learned there was no hope for long-term recovery. But when his daughter suggested I meet with the hospital chaplain I agreed.

A kind-faced, elderly, Catholic priest took me into a private room where he began by asking for the details of my situation. Suddenly I was at a loss. Should I lie to a man of the cloth and say the dying man was my husband? Should I admit to living in what some considered a sinful relationship? Should I just pretend he was a dear friend? Could I pass for a hired caregiver?

Finally, I chose to stick with our lie and volunteered, "My *husband* is Jewish." Totally unperturbed, he went on to offer a nonspecific prayer of succor in a manner that gave me a feeling I was merely a crumb on his daily date-minder. I need not have worried about where I fit in. My tears provided more of a relief.

An Episcopalian by choice, I went to church a few times during Andy's illness, but each time sorrow and sadness overwhelmed me so that I found little solace. What really bothered me was when congregants greeted me, a visitor, after services and solicited the information that my husband was dying and then, the only thing they offered were banalities about him "being OK." I wanted to scream, "No, you don't understand, he really is dying" but, instead, I tearfully excused myself and left.

Later, when Hospice became my daily companion, the doorbell to our apartment rang one day. One of the staff chaplains. From what he said I gathered he was an Evangelical Christian, but I said nothing. Perhaps he'd seen the *mezuzah* on our doorpost and would adjust his prayer routine. At any case, I was emotionally drained and couldn't focus on what I saw as an extra service provided by an organization that was truly dedicated to the dying and their families. Although ours was just one stop of many on his working route throughout our large community, he seemed so sincere when he proceeded to pray like he presumably did with everyone crossing his path, regardless of religious affiliation or choice. Andy was non-reactive in bed so I saw no harm in a different way of praying.

Less than two weeks after he'd returned from the hospital, Passover was on the calendar. There was nothing out of the ordinary progression of the tumor to worry about at that point, and his daughter had returned north for her own holiday. I was filled with the urge to do something to bring spirit into our house so that we could sanctify a central part of his heritage, but since I knew he couldn't last through a traditional seder meal I decided to put together my own service although I'd never done it before. On the other hand, I already knew I could improvise in all areas of my life.

A local restaurant provided the *gefilte fish*, the *matzah ball* soup and the other traditional foods while I baked a flowerless chocolate cake and made my own *Charoset*. Around our large dining room table, we gathered with our only guests, my two sons. Andy happily welcomed them to something he explained he'd done since he was a little boy. His eyes were shining under the black kippah, although the blank look was evidence of already-fading mental processes.

"*Baruch ata Adonai, Eloheinu melech ha-olam…*," he intoned the ancient Hebrew blessings by heart and without any difficulty. My sons looked at me as I joined him.

I opened my *Haggadah*, saved from a consular seder in which I participated years before, and read in English: "We praise You, Eternal God, Ruler of time and space, Creator of the fruit of the vine…."

When we got to the four questions Andy became visibly energized. Although he'd never been able to carry a tune, he loved to sing and now he was anxious to show off his recollection of the old traditions before my sons. Soundly and in his usual off-key voice he broke into the *Ma Nishtana*. I knew then I'd done something good by bringing spirit into his life.

Part-way through the ten plagues, he interrupted, "Let's eat." My sons, anxious to go along with whatever he wanted, said, "Yeah, let's go."

That was the end of Andy's last seder. It was also the beginning of my own awareness that the age-old, Jewish traditions can offer a spiritual connection to the past for a Gentile like me.

As I already said, with the diagnosis came a gradual but noticeable increase in his uncontrollable desire to organize and control his environment, and this meant all kinds of rituals that he simply had to perform to his own satisfaction. One day watching him move papers from one pile and reverently placing them with both hands in another stack, it reminded me of the motions priests – and I'm thinking of the Protestant kind here – go through before they distribute communion to their parishioners. As the tumor raged on, the familiar movements, often endlessly repeated, then assumed the nature of liturgy and I found myself reflecting on what would have comforted me if I were terminal. Prayer, for sure.

Andy may have professed to being an atheist, but he was partially Yeshiva-educated and on his bookshelf thick sterling silver covers held sacred Jewish texts. "Not that you'd understand them," he'd said when he first showed them to me in our new home. "But it's nice to have them here." At that moment, with his cancer diagnosis still fresh on our minds, I wondered if he'd be pulling something from his Jewish traditions if I were dying before him. Would he even consider my feelings when looking for comforting words for me?

From then on, I struggled with that mix of thoughts every time I tucked him into bed.

One night, I suddenly noticed how he'd fallen into a habit of closing his eyes and folding his hands across his chest in a pose of prayer. Acting on some deeply imbedded instinct, or maybe it was my in my genes that one should show respect before a dying person, I knew I shouldn't just assume he wanted me to pray with him. The moment the question tumbled out of my mouth, I was filled with guilt. *Hadn't I promised myself to let him set the tone for his own passing?*

"Yes," came his answer, surprising me both with its strength and its message.

Yes? Did he really want me to pray with him or was his mind so far gone he didn't know what he was saying?

With a bit of hesitation that comes after you regret your impulsiveness, I feigned a cheerful voice as if praying had always been part of our customary bedtime activities. "What prayer would you like me to say?"

"Our Father who art in heaven, hallowed be ...." He started on his own and then his voice trailed off as he haltingly continued to recite the words.

At first, I was too confused to join in. Here was my fiancé, an avowed secular Jew, citing the traditionally Christian prayer, the one Christ supposedly taught his disciples when they asked him to teach them how to pray. As the Gentile in this relationship, what was my role now?

If only I remembered the words to the *Sh'ma*, the prayer that's supposed to be on the lips of every dying Jew, so I could gently guide him through that. Instead, I thought of the apocryphal story about the secular Jew who didn't know what to pray at the Wailing Wall in Jerusalem, so he whispered the

Hamotzi, the blessing of the bread. As those words came pushing through my head I pictured myself giving the familiar blessing, *"Baruch Atah Adonai…,"* but wait.., I'd recently told the old Russians we visited in Moscow that I wasn't Jewish ("no, born in Finland"), so maybe that wasn't right for me either? After all, who was I, really? This person who could spout the ancient Hebrew blessing over the bread, but could not be buried in the same cemetery as her Jewish husband if their romance had, indeed, led to marriage? This *shikse* who loved Jewish comedians and their jokes? This end-of-life caregiver who could easily be replaced by any of the loving Jamaican or Haitian aides so prevalent among the Jewish families in Miami?

It was just too soon to figure all this out.

Four months into Andy's illness I had more pressing matters to think about, as he was now prone to small seizures on a regular basis, and I was learning to physically protect him from injury. These incidents also led him to repeatedly ask, "Why are they picking on me?"

"Who's *they*?" I countered each time, quite Andy-like with his own need for specificity.

And one day he had an answer. When he said, "God wants to hurt me" I thought of how this showed a glimpse of a hidden religious belief system. It seemed right to continue the routine with "Our Father," if only for its calming effect. Clearly, there was no discernible reason why I should've been prompted to change the pattern, but inexplicably I did so.

"Would you like me to say a Swedish prayer?" I found myself asking one evening.

"Yes," came his firm response once again, and I proceeded to recite the age-old Scandinavian plea for God's protection for all of us wherever we are in the world. As happiness comes and happiness goes, the one who loves God will always be content; words rhyming in Swedish but not exactly eloquent in direct English translation. The language didn't seem to matter to Andy, though. He was at peace and that was enough for me. Closer to the end of his life he was sound asleep before I finished the first line, and it was then I knew 'd been able to provide something special for him, something that was familiar and therefore comforting for the dying OCDer.

From Nazi Thugs To The Count's Buses

You wouldn't think movies on World War II and the Holocaust, particularly Frank Capra's graphic documentaries, could be comforting to a dying Jew, but in the case of an OCDer like Andy his life-long obsession with these topics got stronger during the last part of his life. Although we'd watched his vast collection numerous times before, the videos now assumed a central role in our life. The act of sorting and handling them gave him the sense of control that his OCD always demanded, reassuring him that his mind was still grasping important historical facts. Incredible, as it now seems, Hitler and his thugs gave us many moments of lighthearted enjoyment even when Andy increasingly butchered his editorializing of the movies, happily explaining parts of the plot for my benefit.

"That son-of-a-bitch, Reichsmarschall Hermann Göring...," he frequently imitated a German accent. "*She* killed herself."

"Yes, Honey, I know. He's long dead now and it's a good thing." I patted his hand reassuringly. Aphasia had already made it pointless to correct his choice of personal pronouns or add too many details. Simple interactions, although perhaps condescending in nature, gave us countless moments of pleasure. Whatever amount of joy he felt during his dying days was also mine, an unexpected change from the early days of our relationship when I couldn't be in the same room when he was in his Holocaust-mode. Now, I had to admit to myself that his obsession with the horror-inducing topic was all an integral part of the man I loved.

As long as I lived with my parents, they'd nurtured a strong mistrust of Germans although Hitler's was the only country to have come to the aid of Finland against the Soviet threat. Still, the northern scorched-earth policy of the Nazis, when forced by the peace treaty to withdraw from Finland in 1944, left indelible memories with my parents' generation that were frequently passed down to the next. More than a decade after the war, someone my sister and I greatly envied for her good looks and general refinement was still pleading with her parents for permission (although, legally, it wasn't needed) to marry a German diplomat stationed in Helsinki. "Absolutely *no* Germans in our family," they said.

Post-surgery, Andy's obsession with war movies worsened and, although he already owned duplicates and even triplicates of most, I couldn't do anything to stop him from buying more. "We're already here," was his final argument for letting the compulsions rule in a video store. I couldn't see arguing with a dying man and even less so when watching him in front of the TV-screen at home. His delight with the familiar plots and outcomes was comfort in itself. When his daughter visited, all of us watched together – the younger generation, no doubt, learning some history in the process – and after her father's death we split the war movies between us, fully intending to continue watching them all.

One intensely sunny Sunday when we were alone, he was in a contented mood when we enjoyed a leisurely breakfast in our 25th-floor condo with a stunning view of Biscayne Bay. Tentatively, because I wanted to preserve the serenity of the moment, I ventured, "So, what do you want to do with the rest of the day?"

"I like it best when it's only us," he said in a tumor induced non-sequitur. "Just one, two…"

I waited to see if there was any other reaction. His eyes were faraway, with that increasingly blank look caused by a steadily diminishing mind.

"A movie..," he suddenly said and after playing a few lines of the guessing-game I was able to not only narrow it down to Frank Capra's *Nazis Strike* but it was also clear that he wanted to go back to bed to watch it. With a sudden burst of energy, he got up from the kitchen chair and deliberately, although unsteadily, walked to the refrigerator where he grabbed a box of chocolate chip cookies and what I knew as his "secret stash" of Snickers.

And so it was that, on that particular Sunday, close to the end of his life, Andy and I reclined on our beds for three hours indulging in the forbidden pleasure of the sweets his daughter had declared "unhealthy" for him.

"To hell with it," he said in the middle of our feast. "She can't tell me; I do what *I* want!" I was certain he felt in control and that made him happy.

One evening, after watching yet another film on Hitler's relentless march through Europe, he suddenly said, "Sweden was strong." Not sure where he was heading with this unexpected statement, I asked if he wanted to get something from his library about that part of the Holocaust years, but soon it became apparent he wanted *me* to know – as if he hadn't talked about it before the illness – of the two Swedish heroes who'd long intrigued him: Raoul Wallenberg and Count Bernadotte. This, then, became the base for what I'll be including in my talks after Andy's gone:

When Hitler was defeated in Stalingrad (January 1943), Sweden wasn't the only country believing Germany was finally going to lose the war. A natural consequence of this realization was for Swedish government officials to start thinking of its legacy. There had already been criticism of its policy of not doing more to aid its Scandinavian sister countries. As a self-declared neutral nation like theirs, it had continued its trade with Germany and also contributed to Nazi war efforts by allowing Hitler to move troops and military supplies across its "neutral" territory on their way to occupied Norway.

Then there was the pesky matter of the historically close ties between Sweden and Germany, not only the relationship between royals. Ten years after Göring married an aristocratic Swedish lady (after whom he later named his large estate in Germany), the King of Sweden stopped off in Berlin on his way back from his vacation in Italy in 1933, to pay a courtesy visit to Hitler; not in itself unusual between two heads of state, one of whom was the newly appointed Chancellor of Germany. But a letter written in the fall of 1941 to the Führer shows a more effusive king when he thanked "Mein Lieber Reichskanzler" for having decided to "attack Bolshevism everywhere."

After the Nazi fiasco against the Soviets, it'd still be another year before the heroism of Wallenberg in 1944. Although Sweden didn't know it during the years leading up to that time, its humanitarian reputation would get not only one boost but a second one, which was a direct cause by the efforts of the iconic Swede. To understand how this Nordic nation was judged by the world community after the war, we need a better picture of who this man was and how he inspired another mission by a fellow citizen.

Indisputably, there's no Swedish name from the Holocaust years that's more ubiquitous than that of Raoul Wallenberg. After all, there are hundreds, if not thousands, of streets and public squares, and monuments in his name from Stockholm to Jerusalem, from the North and South American continents to Australia. When I give my presentations, I struggle with saying something about him and his rescue efforts in Hungary that wouldn't be a repeat of what I assume my audience already knows.

So, I begin with saying how we tend to idealize dead people who've done a lot of good for causes in which we believe. No wonder that there's a common perception among my listeners that Raul Wallenberg conceived of the rescue idea himself and then, with the poise of a mythical hero, threw himself into saving the Hungarian Jews. So, why have historians described him as *reluctant*? For one thing, he didn't take the initiative to go to Budapest; in essence, he had to be convinced. Here, highlights of his family background and the reasons for the birth of the rescue project provide needed context.

The Wallenberg patriarch, Raoul's grandfather, was a prominent Swedish banker with many special connections throughout the world. He wanted his grandson to get a solid international education, so he was first sent to the University of Michigan (Ann Arbor) where he graduated with a degree in architecture in 1935. His letters home show an adventuresome spirit, for instance how he used to hitch-hike around the US, even as far as to Mexico, without any fear for his safety. An incident with hooligans threatening him with a revolver and, after taking all his money, throwing him out of their car, is often cited as an example of Raoul's sense of dispassion when faced with danger.

Shortly after his graduation, the Nuremberg Laws were enacted (September 1935) to deny German citizenship to Jews. As the persecution of Jews increased and the British administration of Palestine announced a major cut in the permitted quota of immigrants, Raoul was already interning at a bank in Haifa where he personally witnessed the deplorable condition of Jewish refugees. Later, there were rumors, never denied by Wallenberg himself, that he was half-Jewish when, in fact, later researchers put the number at 1/16. Other stories have the family bank buying looted gold from the Nazis, thereby providing additional funds for the German war efforts.

In January 1944, FDR established the War Refugee Board (WRB) to belatedly tackle the situation of "immediate rescue and relief of the Jews of Europe and other victims of enemy persecution." By June of the same year, the Stockholm office put out word that it was looking for a "prominent person, clever, with good reputation, a non-Jew willing to travel to Rumania/Hungary to lead a rescue operation of the Jews." Or, as the head of the agency said, "Someone with good nerves, good language ability" (German and Hungarian).

Coincidentally, a month before this, the chief Stockholm rabbi had ruled out Raoul as a possible candidate to undertake this mission, because he considered the Swedish banker too young and inexperienced. Even his talk about bribes and payoffs turned the old rabbi off, and nothing had come out of the Swede's candidacy at that time.

But now, a chance meeting between the Stockholm head of the WRB and a Hungarian businessman in Stockholm caused Raoul's name to come up again. The latter was looking for help with getting his (Jewish) in-laws out of Budapest, and he knew of Wallenberg's knowledge of the language. Still, Raoul had to be convinced but after this, things happened quickly. The Swede arrived in the Hungarian capital in June of the same year, going straight to work with total dedication and at a great risk for his own life.

A first commitment of $100,000.00 from the Red Cross and the American Jewish Joint Distribution Committee (both with Swiss bank accounts) had been agreed upon, as Raoul knew he was going to need access to a large fund to use with his new local contacts and, in fact, grease the hands of Hungarian officials. Records show that they were often happy to accommodate the Swede when he arranged for "protective passes" (Schutzpasses) for the refugees, claiming they were his conationals or had close business ties to his home country and, therefore, were entitled to leave Hungary. In many cases, both German and Hungarian officials just looked the other way.

Rarely referring to the evacuees as Jews, he said they were humans who didn't deserve to die. He was even seen boarding at least one train scheduled for Auschwitz so he could place needed exit-documents in the desperate hands of the doomed. Because he was affiliated with the Swedish legation, tenuous as that connection might have been, he presented himself as a diplomat with all the privileges attached to that position, although Eichmann told him he wasn't "immune from danger" even as a recognized diplomat.

By the first week of January 1945, Budapest was totally surrounded by the Russians and the trail of the Swede slowly disappears. At this point in my lectures, people usually want to know what happened to Wallenberg since there was still ten months left of the war. Known to be both too trusting and color-blind (not being able to see the red tabs on the uniforms of the Soviet Secret Police) he's said to have gone with the occupying officials for what was assumed (by historians and, maybe also by him) to be a cordial investigation of the situation. Today, it's known that Stalin had an ingrained distrust for someone like Wallenberg, a US-educated capitalist who had been sent to Budapest by the WRB, a suspect American agency. Otherwise, why would a rich Swedish Christian be interested in Hungarian Jews, if he wasn't a spy for Anglo-American interests? This was in itself a good enough reason to have him jailed.

In spite of decades of high-level efforts by the Wallenberg family and others, Raoul never came out of the Soviet prisons alive. It's believed he was executed in Moscow in 1947.

With Wallenberg now gone, someone or something else had to fill the void in terms of Sweden's post-war legacy. This "someone" is Folke Bernadotte and his undertaking with the project of the "White Buses."

White Buses?

Never mind, the name of the Swede associated with the rescue mission named after its mode of transportation isn't as known to my S. Florida audiences as Raoul Wallenberg's. Although a nephew of the sitting King Gustav V, Folke Bernadotte wasn't a prince but, like his ascetic father who gave up the title, he was a count in a country that had long prided itself on its democratic principles of government. Raised in a strict Lutheran household with its daily prayers and Bible reading, he wasn't a man given to introspection or much analytical thought. A dyslexic with little interest in classic literature, he preferred the sacred Christian text or comics throughout his life, while also dedicating himself to the family values of "honesty, obedience, and punctuality." In his memoir, he says the message he got from home was to be of service to others. On his honeymoon with an American heiress of an asbestos fortune (Manville family), he's reported to have told her of his hope to do "something great and honorable" for his country.

The count's royal breeding, combined with the sense of naiveté towards the realities of life that often comes with people who move in the highest circles of society, didn't seem to stand in the way of what one source calls his relentless pursuit of good deeds. In 1937, he became the national Boy Scouts Master of Sweden, and a few years later, when his uncle retired from his post as head of the Swedish Red Cross, he became the natural heir to that prestigious role. Perhaps this is also where he tasted the rewards of public service.

In 1943, a year after assuming the Red Cross position, it seemed like he was the obvious choice for arranging an exchange of German and British POWs. With a lot of fanfare, he oversaw the actual event in Gothenburg, where he got an orchestra to play *Lili Marlene* for the Germans and *It's a Long Way to Tipperary* for the Brits. Some critics said he paid too much attention to stage-managing the exchange; today we'd probably say he was just a micro-manager with natural public relations skills. Either way, it was this event that established Bernadotte as an international force to be reckoned with. Both NBC and CBS put him on their radio broadcast, where he spoke of service to others as being the highest Christian calling.

As I mentioned, Wallenberg's disappearance in January 1945 left a void in Sweden's continued efforts to rehabilitate itself. Still concerned with doing the humanitarian thing, and after the government of Norway (exiled in London with its king) asked the Swedish government for help with saving its citizens, Stockholm officials believed the count was the right choice to lead any additional rescue efforts. In a sense, the new mission began with lists of Norwegians, both Jews and non-Jews, imprisoned in German camps. These were followed by accounts of Danish inmates in Theresienstadt (among them, 500 Jews). Still, without any specific instructions from his own government, Bernadotte was left to his own devices, including bribery, to reach a deal with Germany. Already on record with having said he'd resort to "any means" to save human life and mitigate human suffering, he did, however, caution against talking politics with Nazi officials.

Although it'd been obvious from the beginning of the mission that it hinged on getting access to Himmler, any success depended on concessions from him. Here, there are conflicting versions of how the count managed to arrange for a crucial meeting with Hitler's henchman. While Swedish records showed he had assistance from an intermediary, the identity of this person has been disputed although Felix Kersten, the ubiquitous Finnish massage therapist of Himmler, takes full credit in his memoir for getting his patient to consent to a meeting with the Swede. Meanwhile, there's no mention of Kersten in the count's own memoir.

Since this is not the place to consider the accuracy of dialogues recalled in the original language or in translation, Bernadotte's claim that he got permission to take "all surviving Jewish inmates" (a promise then changed to "take anyone you wish") will have to do. In his memoir he says he understood this to mean he was to save the 13,000 Scandinavians caught in the Nazi camps. There was no mention of the religion or nationality of the internees, although later he was criticized for including every fellow Scandinavian he could find.

More of a direct practical concern was *how* to collect survivors from camps sometimes at long distances from each other, so they could be placed in Camp *Neuengamme* for later pick-up by Bernadotte's rescuers. These assistants were mostly conscripts in the armed services or volunteers, all of whom had to carry their own food and fuel since none of it was available to them in Germany. Any military insignia had to be changed to the emblem of the Red Cross, to show the association with this humanitarian organization providing the needed transportation. To avoid becoming military targets, the legendary buses were painted entirely white (hence, the name of the mission). The roof and the sides had a prominent red cross.

Finally, the first three platoons of twelve buses each, and one platoon of twelve trucks (or nineteen, depending on the source) carrying medical and other equipment, gathered in Southern Sweden for the crossing to Denmark where they were received and fed by that country's Red Cross. On March 12, 1945 the caravan crossed the Danish border to Germany, heading to Neuengamme where they were the first neutral entity to enter into a concentration camp. Here, the goal was to collect the Danish and Norwegian inmates brought there from *Sachsenhausen* (2,200 in number), *Dachau* (600), and other camps (1,600).

Nobody had any illusions about the safety of any of the missions. Typically, Bernadotte rode at the end of the convoy in his private car also painted white with a red cross on the top. He placed an extra driver on the back of the trunk, with instructions to bang on the roof if he heard Allied bombing, so everyone could run for shelter. Still, 16 newly freed inmates were killed during one of three Allied hits. Again, the Swede was criticized, this time for not having taken British warnings seriously.

It must have been quite a sight to see this healthy-looking Viking with his military bearing and dark hair smartly slicked back move around Nazi territory. Today, the peaked hat of the Swedish Royal Horse Guards where he served, makes it seem as if the awkwardly placed cap was too large, or maybe the short visor just makes it seem so. In one picture we see him facing the camera before a group of female inmates in dark winter clothing standing in rapt attention. The caption says "*Ravensbrück* March or April, 1945" although other sources showing the same image tell us this camp first opened its gate on April 24 for 4,000 Jewish females, for transport to Sweden. When I first looked at the photo, my heart sank at the ominous sight of a large X painted across the backs of the coats of these women, as if they'd been marked with the bull's eye of an executioner. Later I learned the opposite was true: these women were the lucky ones.

The end result of the White Buses mission, which continued for two months after Germany's surrender on May 7, 1945, was that approximately 21,000 inmates were saved, 6,500 of whom were Jewish, although numbers again vary from source to source. During an interview in Tel Aviv Bernadotte claimed to have rescued 10,000 Jews, a number some claimed was exaggerated to serve his own self-promoting purposes. Whatever his personal recollections, they were published in Swedish as early as June 15, 1945 in the form of his memoir. In a blunt and concise style, he shares some convictions that have been dispelled since then; for instance, that Hitler was murdered and also that Eva Braun was the prime motivator behind her lover keeping the war going.

As I already mentioned, there's no mention of Himmler's personal masseur, Felix Kersten, whose impact on the Swedish rescue mission still remains a matter of debate among historians. In 1953 (the same year it'd take a heated parliamentary debate in Sweden to finally grant the influential Finn his desired citizenship), a British journal quoted him saying that Bernadotte was *opposed* to the rescue of Jews and that Himmler had said the Swede understood the importance of fighting "world Jewry." The truth behind that particular story has since then been debunked, but it's a telling example of the kind of rancorous material that's continued to feed Bernadotte's detractors.

As I mentioned, the Swedish hero-to-be had his critics from the beginning, mainly among professional diplomats, who considered him inexperienced in the art of diplomacy. They also believed his naiveté could lead to decisions based on bad judgment. A noted historian went so far as to write that Bernadotte's role in the rescue was merely as a "transport officer, nothing more," although he later revised this opinion. Rumors of the Swede being an antisemite still persist, primarily because he'd sheltered a Nazi officer charged with genocide in the Nuremberg trials. Then, there's the loaded quote in the *New York Times*, which has the count saying high-ranking Nazi officers should not be tried if they were merely doing their duty and following military commands.

When I finally get to see one of the buses – I don't remember if the first time was at Yad Vashem in Jerusalem or just in pictures at the many Holocaust centers I've visited – it looks small and boxy with undersized tires that make the chassis almost hug the ground. It's of course white, but somehow it surprises me that the red cross is painted inside a black-edged circle. It's also hard to imagine now how one of these seemingly rickety vehicles could sometimes hold up to fifty inmates, many on stretchers, for a safe transport to Denmark and Sweden.

After the war, in May of 1948, Count Bernadotte was appointed UN Mediator in the Palestinian conflict. Like with his White Buses mission he preferred to travel without any military protection, whole-heartedly believing – but with the innocence he'd been derided for – in the success of the assignment he'd accepted: to bring peace between Arabs and Jews.

On Friday September 17, 1948, a road-block stopped the Swede and his entourage from entering Jerusalem. Hostile signs with "Stockholm is Yours – Jerusalem is Ours" had already greeted him, but the newly-appointed peace negotiator didn't seem concerned. He was there for peace, not war. Presumably, he didn't anticipate the loathing of the men who ambushed his car (later identified as members of Stern Gang). Doctors in the Hadassah Hospital declared Folke Bernadotte dead on arrival.

"By The Time You're A Bride"

Are you his wife? The officious lady in the Records Department of the hospital stared at me intently when I first approached her desk with Andy's written request for a copy of a recent medical test. Upstairs in his room, he'd shown the nurses the big file-folder he always carried with him filled with a complete set of records that came with columns of all his medications, including when and how to take them, and the specific reason for each prescription. Yet, the OCDer in him made him question every dose of medicine brought into his room, so that the nurses had to check them off against his spreadsheet and, once again, explain what each pill was for. Amazingly, none of them seemed to mind it, but rather smiled patiently while complimenting him for being so "organized" and "exact." His childlike innocence always won out over any lack of time or the stress staff might have experienced with anyone else.

When the latest test result went missing from his folder, he buzzed the nurses' desk. With the patience of an angel, one of them said it was available at the Records Department, but he'd have to send his "wife" for it.

There I was, once again playing a role that was never to be mine.

"You his wife?" the Records bureaucrat repeated.

I assumed an equally self-important attitude. "Yes," I said with authority. "I am. My husband, who's upstairs in his room, can't come down himself so he asked me. Would you like to call him to verify?"

"Show me your driver's license. I need proof."

I was beginning to lose my self-confidence but handed her the license with feigned nonchalance.

"This is a different last name!" The clerk sounded elated, as if she'd just caught me red-handedly in a lie that she, astutely, had already anticipated. Then, her tone quickly became accusatory: "You're not his wife!"

My retort was swift: "I'm a modern woman so we use different last names. You must have heard about women like us."

There was a slight pause as she contemplated my status. Then, she turned abruptly and went to photocopy my driver's license. In a few minutes, and without another word, she handed me the report.

"But you *are* my wife!" Andy said after he asked me for the usual recap of a task he'd given me. This was something I'd heard many times during our seven-year relationship but at this point, post-surgery in the hospital, I didn't know if he actually believed what he was saying or if it was just an old habit kicking in. So, I said nothing although the missing marriage had long assumed a disturbing life of its own.

Already during that first night when he lay comatose in Intensive Care, I'd stood by his side struggling with thoughts over my future as a non-wife. *Would I be expected to participate in any medical decisions and, if so, what if I made the wrong one? Maybe Andy's family didn't even want me there, preferring to spend whatever time he'd left without me being around?* Soon I added to my daily worries a growing concern over who I was going to be in the obituary.

What if his children didn't want to include me in the death notice at all? What could I be called at any case? How about "survivor" because that's how I'd be feeling after six months as an unmarried end-of-life caregiver? "Survived by (my name) …" was so insipid that it could be used for a faithful pet or business associate, so that wouldn't do. "A special friend?" "A long-time partner?" Somehow each of those made me feel like a loser, like someone who hadn't passed the imaginary marital test.

A few weeks before Andy was gone, his ex-wife offered to host the *Shiva* at her beautiful apartment in Philadelphia. I was grateful. After the funeral, all I had to do was to show up with my sons. Over bagels and lox, and relieved that the agony of watching a loved one die was now over, I chatted – almost contentedly – with the visitors. And then someone said, "Where's Bev?"

I found her with a book in one of the bedrooms.

"Everyone is asking for you," I said. "Aren't you going to join us?"

"Oh no, *Shiva* is only for the closest members of the family." She barely looked up from her reading material.

There was no answer to my "Where does that leave me, then?" Instead, I had a *déjà vu* of the time when Bev had told me any color went with a Jewish funeral. I left the room and she stayed put.

"You're lucky," the doorman in Andy's Philly apartment building said when I'd flown up for the funeral with my sons. "I remember another owner who died. Him and his lady had been living together longer than you and your Mister, but then his kids changed the locks the next day and she couldn't come in no more. No warning, no nothing."

At least he called me *lady*. A few months later, someone else called me the "ultimate bitch" when she accused me of keeping Andy from his old friends. To my face, with a straight face.

The question about my official status continued to hover around as people didn't quite know how to express their sympathy. Condolences arrived with my maiden name, his last name, or hyphenated versions of both. Always preceded by "Mrs." Some of his friends who were in long marriages, happy or not, had frequently volunteered the obvious solution to a dilemma they felt I shouldn't be left to face. "You can still get married," some of them had told him, but he only scoffed at the idea.

"What for?" he said, puzzled at a suggestion that would've been overwhelming under any normal circumstances but even more so for a closeted OCDer whose cognition was fast diminishing after the initial surgery. I suspected his family didn't support the idea either, because of the fear that a spousal status might have given me an unfair advantage in the estate.

To me, marriage was the gold standard for a relationship between a man and a woman and although "living in sin" was no longer forbidden by society, my personal sentiments mattered much more to me. The only status I had was as "a live-in with a ring" but without a firm wedding date. After Andy's death, I thought, "absolute fool" might also describe me since at that time I'd have to pay the price, literally and emotionally. There were no other accurate words, I whined to an end-of-life psychologist I started seeing during Andy's illness.

I can't say at what point between the diagnosis and Andy's death, I finally resigned myself to the "official" designation of end-of-life caregiver, the do-gooder without a legal status. Living as an unmarried woman with her beloved marching steadily towards an irreversible end had defined me socially as a "good person who doesn't abandon a man in need," but when that man was an OCDer I was already a secret caregiver long before the dying process began. From the lonely life of living the unspoken lie of life with a partner suffering from what was called the Shame Based Disease, it'd take the diagnosis of his terminal illness for me to finally be a "legitimate" caregiver. I was then able to gradually balance the symptoms of his increasingly worsening mental condition – anger, depression, paranoia – with the normal physical demands of any dying person. My only moral obligation became the fulfillment of his end-of-life wishes, as long as they didn't jeopardize his physical well-being.

The literature on caregivers usually talks about spouses and children caring for a dying family member. But what about those of us who give of ourselves just because we're overcome by love? What are we? Are we saints as friends and acquaintances sometimes said, or non-persons as some hospital personnel would intimate? Are we "non-kin caregivers" or one-half of a "romantic couple"? Perhaps the bland "significant other" or the too-legal-sounding "cohabitant," both of which seem the norm today? Could we be "legal strangers" since that's how the law may treat us in case of a death? Maybe we are plain "shack-ups" as the popular radio-host, Dr. Laura (Schlessinger), had said? How about "foolish women living in an immoral relationship?" Or are we, quoting the dying man himself, "wives?"

In the end, I became "life partner" in the obituary, whatever the meaning of that honorific suggested by his daughter. She also shared with me her fear that I'd leave her father when he was diagnosed with the disease we all knew would kill him in a matter of months.

Maybe it was the academic in me that kept obsessing over the different designations, as if I truly wanted to be labelled. Once I was able to shift my focus to the larger purpose of my life, I found comfort in the words from Ecclesiastes, "… a time to be born and a time to die," and for the first time, I began looking at love as a privilege. My ability to love an OCDer was a God-given gift that transcended both of our faults and shortcomings. I was, in fact, lucky to have Andy for a few more months to love and care for.

So, I stayed. A single woman facing an uncertain future. After Andy's passing, there'd be plenty of time to face the practical side of survival. A couple of years into our relationship I'd decided I must become financially self-sufficient by returning to a university position, but this had put him in a nasty mood where he threatened, "That's the end of us." Besides, as he'd been quick to point out, "Who'd ever hire *you*? You're too old."

When we were referred to meet with a psychologist specializing in end-of-life issues, Andy would have nothing to do with her after only one meeting. "What can she do for me?" he said, as I vowed to go by myself, a routine I also continued after his passing. By that time, I was struggling with how it'd been possible for an intelligent, highly educated woman to let herself fall into such a supposedly outmoded trap of defining herself through her man. When the therapist said I'd had choices, I said she was wrong. My lifelong fear had been to be judged a pushy woman or, worse, not a lady of the highest breed (*dignity above all*). So what, that my family had prized the suppression of personal needs at all cost? So what, that guilt had been my guiding light for so long that I genuinely believed my person was less important than Andy's? I was convinced the "choices" the counsellor spoke about never applied to me.

And still, something in me was jolted into the reality I had ignored, willingly or not.

Not that I instantly found my identity, because that was a slow process, but for the first time after Andy's passing I recognized that although society didn't have a word for someone like me, I'd survived both the bad and the ugly of some circumstances I could've controlled. With the help of the therapist, I was beginning to understand how I'd created situations as a distraction from my caregiving duties although, at the time they took place, I'd been devastated. One particular instance stands out:

Half-way through the cancer, a friendly neighbor at our condo complex asked me for a memo to her committee on a situation of little interest to me. During a break in the monotony of caregiving, I gave her my view of the matter, specifically drafted to be inoffensive. But the in-house guerrilla, the kind of condo resident everyone fears, thought differently. When Andy and I returned from a seeing his family for what I knew was his last time, there was a thick stack of papers by our front door. The cover letter to copies of the condo statute said I should be evicted for the moral transgression of living in an unmarried relationship. Hiding the delivery from Andy, I cried silently. Who was this person who thought I was shamelessly immoral, a Jezebel of such proportions I couldn't live in the same community as she? How did she even know I hadn't made it to the altar? Above all, why this now?

Two months after I was left alone, still searching for my identity in a world that didn't seem to have a ready place for me and in an effort to forge a closer connection to my brother, I decided to visit him in the middle of Finland. A little more than two years before, Andy and I had taken a car trip through the country when we stopped for a break at his rural home. Around the kitchen table we sat awkwardly and dry-mouthed for less than an hour, before continuing our journey. The scene reminded me of childhood summer days when an uncle would drop by our cabin unannounced and, depending on the mood of my parents, would get a cup of coffee or not.

Now, an invited houseguest at my brother's by myself for three nights, I was curious to see how we'd manage our frail sibling-relationship.

The first evening, the Swedish sub-titles of the protagonist of some British comedy show moved across the screen of his living room TV. My brother could barely contain his snickering.

"That's Ma all over again," he said.

"Hyacinth Bucket?" I never heard of her before.

"No, that's no bucket …, it's Bouque-et," he said, elongating the end of the French word with heavy sarcasm. "Did you forget mother already? All that phony stuff?"

Even for a TV-ignoramus like myself, it was easy to catch on to the theme of *Keeping up Appearances*. Somehow, the silly English sitcom brought out a bond between my brother and me that we didn't have before. The pretense, snobbery and class distinctions our mother shared with the British protagonist had also made her, quite Mrs. Bouquet-like, call the supervisor of any shop clerk who offended her in some way and, in her steeliest voice, introduce herself before outlining why the service didn't meet her expectations. But while Hyacinth was overbearing and boastful even in large community settings, Finnish social norms had prevented mother from acting that way in public. For the first time I now saw her as a person who tried to assert her personhood just as I was struggling with mine.

Stepping Over The Threshold

It's December of the new Millennium in Miami and with Andy gone for three months, I have 64 toothbrushes to get out of my life. Without my usual glance at the soothing views of Biscayne Bay, I hurry past the floor-to-ceiling bedroom windows to his bathroom where I know these inanimate implements, still in their original packages, are crammed into an aged but barely used canvas kit. I'm determined to conquer his belongings, so I keep repeating to myself that these are nothing more than meaningless machine-made objects and any sensible person would do what I'm about to do.

What if he knows I'm about to throw out what he's spent years accumulating? The sudden thought of him looking over my shoulder makes me tremble with anxiety.

Since he died, I find myself stymied by even the simplest of decisions. Often, I'll spend hours aimlessly surveying the stuff in his bathroom cabinets without touching anything. Mocking me now from their prescribed perches in the bathroom cabinets are shampoos and lotions, baby powder containers and Vaseline jars, pills and deodorants, disposable shavers and bandages, all in scrupulous but tightly packed order, sometimes rubber-banded together by brand

and purpose. With a deep breath to suck in the strength I lack, I make my voice louder than it's been in years.

"This is silly; you've been gone for three months already!" I say.

And then I abruptly return to the familiarity of the toothbrushes.

Maybe it's easier if I keep these for myself... but how many does a person need during a life time... the manufacturers want us to change every six months, so, let's see... with my life expectancy, probably about fifty. Maybe he was right all along..., I could be saving a lot of money here.

My reverie is stopped short when I realize I'm yet again trying to rationalize Andy's obsession with things. Disgusted, I zip up the kit that holds them all and toss it aside. My love for him can't be so powerful that it's trumped the forces of the "proud and fierce independence" long embedded in my genetic code. Or can it?

Maybe I am, after all, just another Scandinavian woman caught on an American stage in a depressing Bergmanesque drama. The director is calling for blind faith in romance and passion but now it's increasingly beginning to look like the props for a life of secret suffering are here. How else to justify the multitude of *things* that continue to control me, now silently watching me flutter from one collection to another, unable to decide what should be done with them?

When I finally manage to turn my back on them I saunter into the hallway where I reach over tightly-packed books, some of them in double rows in the sturdy built-in shelves, to feel my way to a screw-top glass-jar wedged in against the back wall. It holds four keys, each clearly tagged with the closet to which it belongs. I select the one marked "Main closet" and hold it in my palm so long that it starts to feel warm and damp from my sweaty hand. Do I really have the guts to enter the forbidden territory?

When we first renovated the apartment, Andy had a workman put in special locks to all of his closets and, like with every other routine of his, he never failed to lock the doors before putting the keys into a secret spot. I'll never know why, although now I think it was on purpose, but less than a year before his passing, he made a big production of showing me the hiding place.

"Come here; I want you to look at something you'd never figure out on your own," he'd shouted to me then. And in an admonishing tone, "But just because I show it doesn't mean you're allowed to touch it, so don't get any ideas."

I wanted to protest that I didn't want to know where he'd hidden something, but then decided ignorance never worked at any case when he accused "someone" of absconding with things from his closets. No rational argument, such as the fact that only *he* had access to them, made any difference when he was in the throes of paranoia or whatever emotion drove him at the time.

Now I'm happy I'd let him share his hiding place with me.

There's no problem with the key; it slides into the lock as if oiled. This makes me think of the tall WD-40 spray cans with their tiny detachable straw-like squirters which he regularly used on every lock in the apartment and our two cars, and when cleaning his large collection of old and new keys.

In an instant, the door to the closet is open, and I enter with great resolve.

White plastic storage containers in their expensive, customized cubby-holes egg me on to check for their mysterious content. I flip open the lid to the first, expecting to see something I don't already know about him but, instead, I'm strangely disappointed. I've seen his prized assortment of padlocks before, and I know they come in all sizes and makes. There are the usual heavy-duty *Masters* and industrial-size *Medecos* and *Abuses* along with a large heap of inexpensive, no-brand travel-locks hooked into each other as if permanently frozen in some military formation. Still in their original packages are his all-time favorites, the solid steel *Abloys*. "Nobody can tamper with *them*," he'd told me in the authoritative tone he used when talking about things he loved.

Leaning over the sturdy box, no doubt purchased during one of his regular hauls from Costco or Wal-Mart, I ponder what to do next. Each padlock has attached to it the matching keys with duplicates or triplicates hanging from the U-shaped bars, so there's no doubt all of them are still functional, but what can I do with them?

Wonder if anyone has done a study of how many padlocks a person uses during his lifetime... like the toothbrushes but with a gender difference. Can't think of any girlfriend who's ever spoken of locks..., should just hand them out anyway to keep him happy.

Once again disgusted with myself, I snap the top to the box shut and will myself to look around the closet. My eyes get caught in a lineup of meticulously folded plastic laundry bags with their hotel logos all facing in the same direction. Then there are the containers with the vinyl stick-ons from his label-making gadget spelling out contents like "pads," "D-batteries," "plugin nightlights," and "earplugs."

Stacked on top of each other on the floor are two familiar 50-quart containers from his old apartment. I know they're filled with at least 500 little hotel soaps, the lingering fresh scent belying the fact that most of them are dried up and crumbling under the weight of the newer top layers, and the plastic of many of the miniature shampoo, conditioner and lotion bottles is so disintegrated they've leaked on each other. Knowing how much he hated waste, I'd begged him to let me take the newer ones to a home for abused women – particularly after I read about Nancy Reagan collecting hers for that cause – but nothing had convinced him to part with even a handful.

"But you never use these soaps and shampoos...," I tried in a voice that became increasingly weaker and less convincing.

"You don't understand a thing," he shouted more than once.

Again, I didn't know what there was to understand but I did know these rounds with him sapped me of energy. It was easier to tell myself I'd made peace with the supplies. Now the sight of them brings back all the old feelings of inadequacy and defeat, making it impossible to ignore the thought of all the other stuff hidden throughout the apartment. Visions of hotel security chasing after us haunt me when I think of the towels, ash-trays, corkscrews, trays, glasses, cups and stirrers, which were never safe from his kleptomaniac hands when we traveled. One time, while still standing in the lobby after checking out from the Ritz Carlton in San Francisco, the concierge called his name and for an instant my heart stopped. I was convinced Andy had been found out for stuffing a set of bath towels and the robe in his suit case, but instead it was just an affable hotel employee making a big show of wishing us a safe trip home because, as usual, Andy befriended him during our stay. It took the whole cab drive to the airport for my nerves to calm down.

Now, the glaring proof of a life that could have been so different simply won't go away. It's all here right in front of me, pulling me back to the past as if I've no control over myself. My eyes continue to wander from one perfectly organized, but completely packed, shelf to the next, till they rest on a gold-edged circular seder plate lodged upright in a corner. I remember it well. During our first *Pesach* together, I admired the purple and blue hues of this piece of glass with its artfully depicted familiar scenes from Jerusalem and the historical exodus of the Jews. A bright orange *Magen David* was in the center of the plate with its perfectly aligned six indentations for the ceremonial foods. He'd seemed so proud when he told me about spotting it in a Miami Beach gallery, where he'd talked about different patterns with the designer till he finally settled on this. Curious about why he didn't display such a beautiful piece of art, I'd asked him about it.

"What are you? Stupid?" he ranted. "What do you know about Passover and all that talk about the Exodus? It's all nonsense at any case. Did any of it do anything for the Jews in the Holocaust? Tell me! Is that what they taught you in the schools in Finland? You don't know a thing, do you? My parents wanted me in a Yeshiva and what do you think that got me? Nothing, nothing at all." His irrational ramblings, shouted with great intensity, scared me and I wondered then what other reactions he was capable of.

Now I steal a second look at the seder plate and ask myself, "Should I or shouldn't I get rid of it with the rest of his things?" The dilemma is driving me mad. Can it really be I'm still ruled by all those years of accommodating his whims? The thought fills me with shame and self-pity.

Damn him and all his stuff! I'll have every single one of his possessions hauled out of here. That'll show him how crazy he was for having left all this behind!

The sudden jolt to my inherited Nordic stoicism provides welcome relief. Like a petulant child, I want to stomp my foot for emphasis before I'll storm out of the closet in a big show of defiance.

Yeah, that'll really show him.... But then, what? I'm still the one having to deal with all his things. So, who's the crazy one now?

Gingerly, I step over the oak threshold and pull the closet door shut behind me. No more keys, no more locks.

Part 4
The Norwegian Bowler

Naturally, the new grand apartment had to be sold. Andy's daughter was now moving on with her life up north, trusting me to clean out the remaining collections of ..., *everything*. On 9-11, the day that'll be forever on everyone's mind, I walked out of the empty apartment leaving it ready for the final walk-through of the buyer. The nostalgia of the past seven years lay heavy in the air even as I thought of my life going back much longer than that.

Strange how, after a life-altering event, such as the death of a loved one, one has the need to reach out to friends of old. For me, this meant ruminating on the summer of 1967 at the Hague when I made an instant connection with Jon, the Norwegian who took me bowling. He's now a retired judge with a long marriage to a fellow judge.

Although we exchanged Christmas letters each year, I have another reason for contacting him than reliving memories of our shared fun. Although he'd mentioned his grandfather Bonnevie, a distinguished jurist and member of the Supreme Court, I suspect there's more to the story behind that side of the family. And I know Jon will be impartial when giving me details for contextual background because they'll protect against any potential conceit, a characteristic that'd horrify any Scandinavian talking about something personal.

The pride Nordic individuals have in managing life by themselves is clearly summarized in a brief statement from 1942 by the Norwegian Foreign Minister Trygve Lie (in 1946, the first Secretary General of the newly established United Nations). When the British Section of the World Jewish Congress asked him about the welfare of the Jews in Norway (the Wannsee Protocol count was 1,300), he said there was no need for his government to make a special appeal to the general population because his fellow citizens would "fulfill their human duty towards the Jews of Norway." No outside help needed or wanted.

It's not necessary for me to remind Jon, although it's a timely repeat for readers and listeners, that Hitler invaded Norway and Denmark on the same day, April 9, 1940. But in contrast to what happened in Denmark, which held a favored position in the Nazi plan (more on that later), the resistance movement in Norway sprung into immediate action, sabotaging factories and strategic ports. The goal was also to damage German war ships to prevent their access to the production sites of heavy water needed in the race for the atomic bomb.

As was the practice in other Nazi-occupied territories, the persecution of Jews began by mandatory registration. Although an immediate prohibition against owning radios was put in effect for the overall population, the underground used the airwaves to stay informed about impending threats so Jews could go into hiding or embark on the illegal crossing across the border to Sweden. Still, in October 1942, 300 Jewish males were arrested and sent to a Norwegian concentration camp, which also housed some military officers waiting for their deportation orders. Eventually, a total of 767 Jews (again, numbers vary) was deported, primarily to Auschwitz. Only 26 survived.

When Jon and I finally talk about the war years in his home country, he begins his story with the letter *bestefar* (the Norwegian epithet for grandfather) sent to Vidkun Quisling, a fellow citizen, whose last name would instantly go down in history as a synonym for traitor (thanks to a lead story in the British *Times* on April 15, 1940). His unusual act of treason began in the evening of the first day of the occupation when Quisling went on the airwaves to declare himself prime minister, an act that's later been called the world's first coup d'état by radio.

Bestefar listened to the speech and waited a month till May 3, 1940, when he in his capacity as a Supreme Court Justice, asked Quisling to explain why he should not be charged with treason. There was no reply to the written request. And soon, the self-proclaimed government leader fell out of favor with the Nazi occupiers as it became clear he was incapable of dealing with the civil unrest breaking out all over the nation.

Teachers, who were refusing to work under Nazi authority, resigned *en masse*, and Lutheran clergy – also state employees – who didn't want to toe the party line by sermonizing about Nazi virtues in the Third Reich, held their own services for like-minded congregants who far out-numbered the one or two souls who visited the "Nazi church." There were continued strikes, much of it set in motion by a highly active underground committed to sabotaging anything that could benefit the German war efforts.

Observing Quisling's failure to maintain order, and less than a month after he took the office of government leader, the Führer sent Reichskommissar Josef Terboven to get control of the reluctant country. Contrary to Denmark which, some believed, gave in to the Nazi occupiers without a fight, the Norwegians actively resisted for three months. Another difference between the two nations was that while the King of Denmark remained in Copenhagen throughout the war, King Haakon of Norway and his family members and cabinet fled to London, where the government-in-exile continued to function under the nation's constitutional provisions.

Under Terboven, the civilian administration, including all the courts, was quickly put under German control which immediately set a mandatory retirement age of 65 for all Justices of the Supreme Court. The Nazi plan was obvious: by lowering the age from 70, the occupiers wanted to load the Court with Norwegians friendly to the new regime.

Bestefar couldn't stomach the thought that his beloved constitution, modeled on the US and French founding documents and adopted in 1814, was being so obviously violated, although the Justice and his fellow members of the court had expected as much. Wherever there was Nazi occupation, the ancient democratic doctrine of separation of powers was eliminated and the laws of the oppressors unrelentingly enforced. In the case of Norway, an earlier ban on Jewish entry into the country – but abolished since 1851 – was simply re-enacted.

Six months after Grandpa Bonnevie's letter to Quisling, one of his fellow Justices was arrested in November of 1940. And then, less than a month after that incident – on December 21, 1940, to be exact – he and the remaining colleagues took the brave step of showing their opposition to the occupation leaders by simply walking away from their positions on the highest court of the land. This was not an act they took lightly because they knew their future was at stake, perhaps even their lives.

Although *bestefar* wasn't arrested for his act of defiance, he was now without employment. In his journals from the war, he wrote about this period how he had to depend on loans from wealthy friends to put food on the table for his family. As Jon told me, for the respected, previously self-sufficient jurist, this was quite a humiliating experience. But still, there's nothing in his personal papers explaining why he did what he did a little less than two years after he first asked Quisling to explain why he shouldn't be tried for treason.

This time around (on February 11, 1942) he sent a letter to the Ministry of Justice complaining about Quisling. Instead of being ignored once again, *bestefar* was promptly sent to prison, where he lingered for more than a year. To me, this sounds like an expected outcome wherever Nazi Germany became the occupying force. So, I'm curious about the reaction of the Justice's wife, Jon's grandmother.

"What about your *mormor* Margrete?" I ask, using the Swedish word for grandmother. "It couldn't have been easy on her either, although I know she was a strong woman in her own right."

"Oh, she was furious with him," Jon says. "She said she told him over and over again he was setting himself up for arrest and possible execution by challenging the Nazis, but he wouldn't listen. She never understood why he did what he did."

It surprises me that she wasn't able to convince her husband not to take on the Nazis, because she looked like an assertive woman on the newspaper picture Jon had shown me at the Hague. Not an actual photograph, it was instead a faded tobacco ad from the 1930s. In this, she – Jon's bestemor, as he called her in Norwegian – sits in front of what looks like a shelf of law books, noticeably holding a cigarette in her right hand. Dressed in a black outfit with a white petal-like collar, she looks utterly self-confident. It's impossible for me to picture this woman unable to keep her husband from confronting the Nazis at great risk for his life. Not even a vase of flowers next to Grandma Bonnevie manages to soften the look of a female pioneer with a purpose. Two decades later she's to publish one of her many humanistic books, *Fra mannssamfunn til menneskesamfunn* (From a society for men to a society for people), an inscribed copy of which Jon promptly sent me after we both return home from the Hague.

Around the time when Grandpa Bonnevie was jailed for defying the Nazi regime (in 1942), the famous American novelist John Steinbeck was penning a short novel to boost the morale of people who resisted tyranny. *The Moon is Down*, a line borrowed from MacBeth, expressed his conviction that democracy can only be temporarily down, as it's supported by individuals who treasure their freedom. Originally set in a fictitious American location, the place was soon changed to a small port town described as, "Cold and stern like Norway, cunning and implacable like Denmark." The common belief was that this was the Norwegian *Narvik* from where the Germans shipped iron ore purchased from Sweden.

It's no surprise, then, that the pro-democracy propaganda theme made the Nazi occupiers quickly ban the book. However, printers in Sweden were able to produce tissue-thin copies that were then smuggled back into Norway where members of the underground risked their lives to spread the novel's message of hope.

From Oslo, the manuscript traveled to Copenhagen where two law students translated the text to Danish. As the story goes, they finished it in a week with the Oxford English dictionary in one hand and a glass of beer in the other. A third student then borrowed money against his life insurance policy to purchase a copy machine for the bookstore he owned and managed on the ground floor of the same building as the headquarters of the German secret state police, the Gestapo. With people coming and going at all times of the day to and from the Nazi office, he didn't arouse any suspicion when his fellow students came by to pick up bundles of the book. In fact, he brazenly asked Gestapo agents for help with loading the trucks. "Don't just stand there. Help these kids," he's quoted as saying to the nearby Nazis.

One month after this Steinbeck novel appeared in America, it became a play on Broadway. A year later it opened in a London production, supported by the presence of the King of Norway. In 1943, it was also made into a film. The book went on to lead a long life in innumerable editions, even in far-flung languages like Russian and Chinese. What had started out as a propaganda piece for the US Government – and although it was criticized for being too soft on the Nazis, if indeed these were the unnamed occupiers in the text – also gave an undeniable boost to the resistance in other countries like Holland and Italy, in addition to already mentioned Norway and Denmark.

In 1945, both countries were liberated. Only one of the Norwegian Supreme Court Justices, Paal Berg, would be heralded as a war hero for his leadership in the resistance movement. There's no telling what reaction Grandpa Bonnevie would have shared publicly if he were still alive in 2012 when the late Berg had attracted so much fame that a Norwegian writer even contacted Jon for more insight into this former colleague of his *bestefar*.

With typical modesty Jon didn't volunteer to the author that his grandmother didn't only have her husband's life to worry about. She also had a son (Jon's uncle) whose activism had gotten him arrested for possession and distribution of what the Nazi government called an "illegal paper." For that, he was shipped to the *Sachsenhausen* concentration camp outside Berlin, where he eventually was saved by the Bernadotte rescue mission.

"If it hadn't been for the White Buses, he wouldn't have survived the war," Jon says matter of fact.

As he and I continue to reminisce, I ask if he remembers his first experience with the Jewish Question. His socially prominent family, although well-informed about the deportations, didn't know of any Jews in their social circles. It wasn't until Jon was 13 and transferred to a new school when he sensed an emerging semitic awareness. That's when he got a new homeroom teacher who was also his instructor in German, a man with the non-Norwegian-sounding name of Oscar Mendelsohn.

This man never spoke to his students about the war or his own experiences. Jon told me he learned from overhearing his parents that this man was a Norwegian Jew who'd lost his parents and oldest brother in Auschwitz. These discussions in his home, sometimes spoken in whispers and sometimes with words that Jon couldn't yet understand, were his initiation in the subject of persecution and extermination of the Norwegian Jews.

"When I learned how my teacher escaped to Sweden in 1942 and then came back to Norway when the war was over, I remember how excited I was. It was all like a thriller – almost like an American cowboy movie – although I could tell from my parents' voices that with Mendelsohn this was something very different," he told me.

"You're talking about the Mendelsohn…?" I say. "The one whose name is forever attached to *Jødenes historie og liv i Norge gjennom 300 år* (The History and Life of Norway's Jews through Three-Hundred Years)?"

Jon is quite impressed that I know of this tome by his former teacher. I must explain myself. After Andy died, when boxing carton after carton of Holocaust books, I'd noticed there was nothing in his collection on the topic of the Norwegian Jews. Later, when I researched that area I learned of the Mendelsohn *magnum opus*, immediately wanting to add it to my own reference library. I was thrilled when another Norwegian friend, not Jon, reported he'd found a copy in a used bookstore in Oslo. Did I want him to lay out US$195.00 on my behalf? A week later, after mulling it over, I'd given him the OK. Another week went by before the letter arrived from my friend: copy long gone. Worse, antiquarians told him it was nowhere to be found.

"I wish I'd known there was a connection between him and you, then maybe

I wouldn't have hesitated so long to buy his book but I only knew of Mendelsohn as a respected Norwegian academic and writer," I say to Jon. "By the way, I read somewhere he was knighted by the King of Norway in 1989; one of a small number of Jewish knights throughout Scandinavia."

"Naturally, I also thought $195.00 was a lot of money for my personal non-academic library," I add. "All I can hope now is that the copy I should've bought ended up in the hands of serious scholars or researchers, rather than in the hands of a private person who wouldn't treasure it like it should be, or, who knows, much worse, a revisionist historian."

"You wouldn't need it at any case. It's much too detailed for your purposes," Jon says in the reassuring voice I remember so well from our youthful, virtuous times in the summer of 1967 at the Hague. "Wouldn't you rather hear individual stories about Norwegians with great moral courage…?"

"Like Grandpa-Justice Bonnevie," I say.

"Yes, and to think that somewhere in America my bestefar is still being talked about," he says. "Strange how it all began with that Swedish-speaking girl from Finland who went bowling with me in Holland. *Hvem hadde trodd?* Who'd have thought?"

"We Have No Plan"

I can't say exactly why, but I've taken to conducting an imaginary "survey" of the countries generating the most interest, usually expressed in questions by my listeners. In my mind, Denmark is still in the undisputed first position (something I noticed in my early years in Miami, where any talk about the Jews in wartime Denmark had first surprised me), while second place isn't as easy to judge. For sure, Norway can be an equal contender for the number two spot with Sweden, but it can also be an unquestionable third in line of interest. Either way, Finland is in the last place unless, of course, I've been specifically asked to make it my main focus and even then, questions and comments arise on Jews in other geographic areas, including as far away as Hungary.

Still, the shared history between all the Nordic countries makes it impossible to totally disregard one in favor of the other. There are both overlapping activities and distinctions; we need only think of the Swedish proclamation of its own neutrality while continuing to trade with Nazi Germany, and how Denmark and Norway were the only two Scandinavian countries occupied by Hitler, leaving Finland in its peculiar position of co-belligerence with him.

I also notice an unmistakable trend among my listeners, whether in a lecture venue or social setting: many are more anxious to share what they believe is a fact of history, as opposed to asking a question about it.

"Aah, the king who wore the Yellow Star in solidarity with the Jews," someone says – *tells* me – as if I might previously have overlooked this piece of information.

"Did you know, the *whole* Jewish population in Denmark went underground overnight?" another says.

Regardless, some of the later media coverage of the rise in global antisemitism often comes with the predictable references to the wartime Danes and the Jews. Or the king and the star. But, as we've seen, to fully appreciate the truth it's good to put human faces on the drama played out among the Jews all over Scandinavia, and that's what I gradually started doing in my lectures.

As I said, but it calls for yet another repetition, the invasion of Denmark began on the same infamous day of April 9, 1940 when Hitler also invaded Norway. But while the latter country relentlessly fought the Nazi occupiers, the Danes capitulated without a fight. Because Nazi Germany needed farm products and the Danish population had long been considered close to Aryan ideals, Hitler quickly established what historians came to call a political laboratory. Even his chosen term for his new possession – a "protectorate" – was designed to show the world that cooperating countries could live in peace under Nazi rule. London used a more derogatory description for the arrangement – "Hitler's parakeet" – a euphemism from the mining world where these birds were used to test for escaping poisonous gases that, if unchecked, would kill miners.

Call it what you wish, the new Nazi experiment in Denmark left the control of the occupied territory in the hands of its king. It's been suggested that he continued to take his daily morning-ride through the streets of Copenhagen on his horse. Alone. Without any royal guards. Even by the standards of that time this seems implausible both within acceptable royal protocol and the usual wartime activities. Still, that part of the king's courage, true or not, lives on.

He also showed an early dedication to the safety of the Jews, a well-established part of Danish society since the early 17th century and now with the added number of those who'd fled persecution in Russia, Poland, and the Baltic countries. Moreover, at least 10,000 young Zionists arrived from Germany and

Austria between 1933-1938, all intending to learn about Danish agriculture before emigrating to Palestine where those skills would be applied to building the new state.

Long before the occupation, the king told members of the Copenhagen synagogue he was honored to come celebrate its 100th anniversary with them. In fact, this promise would make him the first-ever member of the Danish royal house to enter a Jewish house of worship. But since this was the same year Hitler was appointed Chancellor of Germany (1933), some in the Jewish community, including the chairman of the congregation, thought it was only right to give the king an opportunity to back out of his commitment to attend. Without any hesitation or consultation with royal advisors, the response by King Christian was, "Are you out of your right mind, man? Now, of course, is when I shall be going!" This is the same king who'd later send a hand-written letter of support to Rabbi Melchior in Copenhagen after an arson attempt to destroy the synagogue, and who also reached into his own pocket to pay for the damages.

With the king on the throne during the German regime, enforcement of domestic law was still kept in the hands of the Danish police, so saboteurs, for instance, weren't punished through routine Nazi executions. Although rationing was in place, inventive Danes found a way to keep life as normal as possible. Jews and Christians moved freely around on their bicycles or by foot, just like in the children's book I'll be describing a little bit later. And, like in the rest of Scandinavia, ubiquitous seaside cottages provided a dependable summer-break from worries about the war. Little did the owners of these little homes on the water know then about the role their cabins would play in the rescue of their Jewish countrymen.

But not even the king himself could contain the confluence of events that drastically changed the Danish situation. When in 1942, news spread from Finland, the eastern neighbor across the water, about two visits by Himmler, Jews throughout Scandinavia took this as a bad omen as rumors spread about their lives being in imminent danger since butchering always seemed to follow the leader of the terror-inducing SS.

Also, in the same year there was the botched matter of a seemingly insignificant piece of international diplomatic protocol, which added to Nazi worries about containing any Danish unrest: the traditional exchange of greetings between two heads of state. It was in September when Hitler flew in a rage over the situation in his model protectorate because he'd sent birthday greetings to King Christian, who then responded with a curt "I thank you" instead of the warm and effusive note the Führer had expected.

Just two weeks later, there was another event leading to Hitler tightening the controls over his Denmark: the king fell off his horse and sustained such extensive injuries that he had to transfer his powers temporarily to Crown Prince Frederick. While the Führer had generally held the king in high regards, the young prince was an unknown entity. When the Copenhagen synagogue was painted with swastikas and arsonists tried to set it on fire once again (in 1942), the Nazis used it as evidence that the Danes, instigated by the Jews, were getting ready to rebel.

An increase in the amount of sabotage was the excuse needed for propaganda purposes. The Germans simply claimed these acts couldn't have been committed by the non-Jewish Danes, who were "too loyal, too cooperative and too Aryan" to have done so. Once again, the Jews were blamed. The period of what's often been called the "peaceful occupation" finally came to an end in August 1943 when martial law was declared throughout the country. Among all, this meant the Nazis were now arresting civilians, Jews and non-Jews alike, including Danish military personnel.

It wasn't until after the war when we learned there'd only been 89 German officials in place to keep the 3.9 million Danes under control (by way of comparison, the number for Norway, with a population of only 3 million and an active resistance movement, was 260). In retrospect, it now seems that a revolt by a united people might have been successful against the Germans, but of course, that's only speculation.

As the Nazis took military control over governmental functions, the king proclaimed himself a "prisoner of war." Although he'd declared there was no Jewish Question in his country, the Jewish community was beset by rumors of a Nazi roundup although several cries of wolf (that the Germans were coming for the Jews) had made some of the population so apathetic they didn't believe the eventually timely warning of impending Nazi arrests. Some even argued it was safer to remain under German rule than to flee the country.

A roundup of all Jews was set to begin on the first day of Rosh Hashanah, the Jewish New Year, on September 30, 1943. About 1,300 Gestapo agents were ready with a list of Jewish residences stolen from the Copenhagen congregation by a Danish Nazi. Because the Germans didn't want to jeopardize the flow of agricultural and other products from Denmark, their instructions were not to enter a Jewish residence by force – thereby risking a negative effect on the much-needed provisions by the Nazis – but to knock politely on the front door. Naturally, this gave extra time for families to flee through back doors and neighboring alleyways, often with the help of accommodating fellow Danes.

On the eve of the holiday, congregants at the main synagogue in Denmark were expecting the traditional sermon, although the official chief rabbi had already been interned a month earlier in a camp outside Copenhagen with about 100 prominent Danes, including twelve Jews. Instead, their acting chief rabbi, Marcus Melchior opened with an extreme statement. "There will be no service today," he said. The Germans were planning to arrest all Jews the following day when everyone was expected to be in their homes or at their synagogues. "By nightfall, we must all be in hiding," he went on.

As rabbi repeats in his memoir (published in 1968), "We have no plan." Instead, he added, "You must leave the synagogue now and contact all relatives, friends, and neighbors you know who're Jewish." He also advised his congregants to ask all their Christian friends and neighbors to spread the word to any Jew they knew. Indeed, history confirms that "regular Danes" from civil servants to shop owners and teachers volunteered in the improvised rescue efforts. "It was exactly the same as having your neighbor's house on fire," they said. "It was the natural thing to do." The press later chimed in with its observation that it was simply impossible to separate the Jews from Danish cultural traditions, while writing such things as "a Dane is a Dane, and nobody comes between us."

With no formal plan in place at first, an informal idea soon evolved. Since herring season was in full swing, the strait between Denmark and Sweden was filled with row boats and fishing vessels loaded with fish nets and other nautical equipment that could serve as cover for the refugees. Gestapo agents guarding the coastline sometimes even looked the other way when seeing an unusual number of small vessels passing by. There can only be speculation for the motives behind this inertia.

The main problem with this plan to get the Jews – mainly from Copenhagen where most of them lived – to Sweden, was that they'd have to hide out somewhere on the coast till a seaworthy craft of some sort was found to take them across the water. Here, the ever-present Nordic summer cottages played a vital role as natural but temporary escape points, although sometimes fleeing Jews found these seaside dwellings boarded up for the winter. Wartime diaries, eyewitness accounts and post-war interviews recount stories about notes or money left by these refugees apologizing for the damage they caused when they had to break a window to enter the only safe place they could find.

History is also replete with the ingenuity and cooperative spirit of ordinary Danes who participated in the arduous process of first identifying Jews and then smuggling them to their seaside departure points and across the water to Sweden. Some residents went through local phone books looking for Jewish-sounding last names to be called with the alert to leave. Staged funeral processions and ambulance transports were also common. Pharmacists handed out drugs to sedate children. Hospitals released their Jewish patients, only to readmit them under Christian-sounding names, frequently taking in perfectly healthy Jews just to keep them safe in an infirmary.

There's an amusing story by an eyewitness to a German Gestapo agent who went to one of the hospitals to inquire about a patient who seemed suspiciously Jewish to him.

"What's the matter with him?" said the Nazi. "Oh, he has the German Measles," was the sardonic response of the Danish warden. At that time, this was a highly contagious, viral infection, so the Nazi quickly left without catching on to the subtle Danish humor.

Even the Lutheran clergy became active participants in the rescue efforts, when the bishops, a few days after the planned roundup, dispatched seminary students to carry a letter to all churches in the land for congregants to hear the pastoral message, which partly said, "The Christian Church is duty-bound to protest against this action." Pastors also routinely handed out blank baptismal certificates to be completed by the refugees. A Lutheran minister was the first to give shelter to Rabbi Melchior, who later moved to the home of a Christian farmer who, when learning of rabbi's kosher regimen, made sure the household respected the religious leader by observing the same dietary rules throughout his stay with them. It's clear from rabbi's memoir how this incident strengthened his devotion to his countrymen whom he credited, along with the king, for his own survival and that of his *landsmen*.

Naturally, there are also stories about reprehensible events. One in particular is frequently repeated because it involved a seaside church where a group of eighty Jews took refuge while waiting for a suitable skipper to be found for the transport to Sweden. Since centuries-old Scandinavian law and tradition treat churches as a sanctuary from invading marauders, it makes it even more appalling to consider how a local Danish girl gave away the hiding place of these refugees, all of whom were killed. We can only guess at her motivation, although some stories claim she was in love with a German Nazi.

Other incidents that can only show humans in their fallible state describe how Jews sometimes were over-charged for their transport, although we also know of gentile Danes who either refused payment for services or offered them at greatly reduced rates. More importantly, nobody was left behind for not having enough money for the fare.

The Nazis were so sure of their success that they had ships (the *Wartheland* being the best known) waiting to take thousands of prisoners to a concentration camp in Germany. After the first roundup of less than 300 Jews left the first transport vessel and another one nearly empty, the news about their departure so enraged Hitler that he sent Eichmann to Denmark to correct the bad situation. After the war, during his hide-out years in Buenos Aires, Eichmann said in a November, 1960 interview in *Time* Magazine – later confirmed during his Jerusalem trial – that Denmark was one of the biggest failures of the Nazi regime and how this continued to infuriate him for the rest of his life.

Since there was no requirement for Danes to register with their religious affiliation (the same was – still *is* – true of it and the other Scandinavian countries), historians can only make educated estimates about the Jewish population leading up to the roundup. The Danish column of the 1942 *Wannsee* Protocol, the record used by the Nazis in their planning of the Final Solution, showed 5,600 but this number fluctuates with other source materials, up to an estimate of 8,000. By way of contrast, Finland was listed with 2,300, Norway with 1,300, Sweden with 8,000, and Estonia had been declared "judenfrei" (free of Jews). At the meetings, one of the Nazis had floated a proposal that all the Scandinavian countries should be excluded from consideration, because the Nordic people were considered fellow Aryans who could be dealt with after Hitler won the war. In the end, all were included in the Protocol.

The final number of arrested Danish Jews is commonly said to be 472, but even this number varies slightly from source to source. Generally speaking, those who didn't go into hiding overnight and therefore were caught in the Nazi claws were those elderly and infirm who couldn't be moved on time. Others left behind were those who simply refused to leave their homes because they just couldn't believe, after three years of living in a "model protectorate," that this roundup was going to be real.

All arrestees were sent to *Therezienstadt*, the shameful "model camp," where internees were made to perform in surreal roles of happiness and contentment during a disgraceful visit on June 23, 1944 by the International Red Cross. Although the inspecting group was augmented by personnel from Denmark, the Nazi hosts were able to convince Danish officials all was well in the camp and there was no mistreatment of the Jews.

The King(s) And I

On June 5, 1963, the *Tuscaloosa News* (Alabama) ran a small notice about a double-death that had taken place an ocean away, in a Danish "nerve clinic" called *Skodsborg badesanatorium* (today, we'd call it a spa) in an isolated area 10 miles north of Copenhagen. A nurse made the grisly discovery early in the morning when she went to check on the couple she already knew as her patients.

Charlotte Kauffmann, the wife, had slit the throat of her 74-year old husband Henrik with a bread knife. Then she took her own life, although the newspaper clip doesn't say how. The bodies were next to each other and with them was a letter explaining the reason for their demise: Henrik suffered from inoperable prostate cancer and his 62-year old wife didn't picture a life without him. The Alabama paper called the gruesome finding a mercy-slaying.

The dead man was an aristocrat who'd been Denmark's Ambassador to the US from 1939 to 1958, working and living in Washington, DC. As opposed to a consul, who normally doesn't have direct access to the president of the country where he serves, an ambassador is the personal representative of one head of state to another. As such, Kauffmann had, in fact, been the main spokesperson for his country in the United States, serving as King Christian's personal envoy to three American presidents (Roosevelt, Truman, and Eisenhower) for almost two decades.

Cutting quite a figure in his impeccably tailored suits and bow ties, he was often described as flamboyant, although it's hard to call up that image when looking at old pictures. Stately seems a more fitting word. Besides, his diplomatic duties required a strict dress code when he moved in the highest social circles boosted by not only his personal friendship with FDR but his marriage to the daughter of American Rear Admiral McDougal.

But on Tuesday April 9, 1940 life changed for Ambassador Kauffmann. He was awakened in Washington by the news that Nazi Germany had carried out what was called a "peaceful occupation" of his home country. As we saw earlier, the king was allowed to remain as head of the government, seemingly unafraid of the growing presence of Germans. It wasn't long before the Nazis demanded Kauffmann, the king's hand-picked envoy at Denmark's Washington embassy, be replaced with an ambassador friendly to their regime. But he refused to leave his post. He told the occupiers back home that he was the only legitimate spokesperson in the United States for the king because there was no such concept under international law as a "peaceful occupation." He even went so far as to urge all Danish consuls across America to follow his example. When they, too, informed the home office in Copenhagen they weren't about to leave their posts the Nazis simply dismissed them. Kauffmann also asked his fellow ambassadors of Denmark around the world to remain in place, but it seems only the Danish envoy to Iran followed suit.

For the rest of the war, Kauffmann remained the only prominent Danish official to publicly condemn any kind of cooperation with Nazi Germany. Even a charge of high treason didn't stop him from his diplomatic rounds through Washington, all the time continuing to nurture his close friendship with President Roosevelt.

On the first anniversary of the German occupation, Kauffmann again did something unheard of in international law and diplomacy. On April 9, 1941, he signed a secret agreement "in the name of the [Danish] King" with Cordell Hull, Roosevelt's Secretary of State, whose advice in 1939 to FDR had resulted in over 900 Jews on the ship MS St. Louis being denied entry into the US. Although not addressing the Jewish Question, Kauffmann's treaty, once approved by President Roosevelt, meant that America had the right to build military bases in Greenland, a strategically important self-governing Danish territory in the Atlantic, between Europe and America. Back home in Copenhagen, government officials operating under the rules of a "hostile government," as Kauffmann so succinctly put it, promptly declared the treaty null and void. This didn't seem to bother Denmark's signatory of the agreement, the man on whom delighted Greenlanders soon bestowed the title of King of Greenland.

Even before the Nazi invasion of his home country, Kauffmann had been visited in the Washington embassy by a spokesman for the World Jewish Congress, who shared rumors about camps and extermination. Later, as Danish funds were frozen in the US, Kauffmann still had access to several accounts and, as he told the Swedish Minister in Washington, Denmark was therefore ready to give financial assistance to Jews fleeing to Sweden. He also went on to inform Secretary Hull that the offer was extended to any other country for costs incurred with giving Danish Jews shelter. Kauffmann's colleague, Denmark's envoy in London, called the deal "a bit premature," as if there ever was a perfect time for reaching out with an offer of support. He seemed to scoff at the whole idea of monetary assistance when he wrote in his journal that there hadn't been any persecution [of Jews] "yet."

How quaint this kind of naiveté seems today as history shows how the torment of Jews in all occupied countries began with lesser measures, such as the requirement for registration and the abandonment of their properties, all of which peaked with camps and extermination. Although the "peaceful occupation" of Denmark never resulted in a demand for the Jewish population to wear the Yellow Star, we've already seen the progression to a roundup. Escaping to Sweden was the only solution, and if Kauffmann could tap into Danish funds in America maybe he could ensure no refugee was left behind for lack of money.

In spite of his good intentions and his success in getting access to the frozen Danish assets in the US, Kauffmann had a real PR-problem on his hands. When word spread among the American public that his country had so quickly given in to the Nazi invaders – or as some in the media put it, "cooperated" with Hitler

– he vowed to show the world the goal of his beloved homeland was to be liberated. Although the press had given some coverage to the brave Danish sailors who volunteered with Allied forces to keep the lines open to vital supplies, more goodwill was needed. Just like his Greenland Treaty created good publicity, Kauffmann's decision to participate in the fund-raising efforts of the World Jewish Congress could only benefit the cause. And, as I wrote earlier, Bernays, the public relations professional working behind the scenes for the Denmark-America Association, also helped the country present a positive public face to the world.

Henrik Kauffmann remained in his ambassadorial post till after the War. When the United Nations was created in San Francisco in 1945, it was he who stood in for Denmark. He didn't permanently return to his homeland until his retirement in 1958. Five years later, when word of his gruesome death reached the Greenland media, there was wide-spread grief.

Today, the Danish and the US flags fly side-by-side at the Thule Air Force Base in the still-Danish territory. Although I've visited Greenland three times, I've not seen a memorial to Henrik Kauffmann, the diplomat who should be remembered for his public stand against Hitler. Also, his name isn't in Yad Vashem among the ten Righteous Gentiles from Denmark, perhaps because one of the criteria for the award is a "risk to the rescuer's life, liberty or position." While Kauffmann was safely doing his work in America, he didn't face any direct danger of losing his life or liberty. As long as the president – first Roosevelt, then his successors – recognized him as the legitimate envoy for Denmark his "position" was also not in danger. The Nazi occupiers of his homeland would obviously disagree.

During my years of talks on the Danish situation, I've yet to meet somebody who's heard of Kauffmann. Even as the king is often quoted for his bold statement, "There are no Jews, only Danes," we should remember that courage and integrity also belong to others who, through their actions, lend a human face to the overall drama. This is reason enough for me to include the King of Greenland.

But whatever choices we speakers make, we must also make sure that the anecdotes we share are grounded in relevant historical facts (even when the best sources are inconsistent with each other, or plainly wrong). Because our stories are not static, they'll continue to evolve as new research comes to light.

In more recent times, I find myself including in my Danish talk-segments the names of two German Nazis who played a pivotal role in the rescue-scenario: Reichskommissar Werner Best (Hitler's civilian administrator of Denmark, also known as "the Bloodhound of Paris"), and Georg Duckwitz, a German diplomat with the unusual talent of having total command of the Danish language, a skill he acquired in pre-war times in Denmark.

Depending on the source one consults, one of these two confidants – or possibly both – put in place by Hitler to take charge of the roundup should be credited with giving advance warning to a Danish politician of the upcoming arrests of the Jews. At the beginning of my early readings, I didn't know how to judge the truth behind someone's boastful journals and later revisionist tales, and since both Best and Duckwitz claimed credit for saving the Jews of Denmark I had to leave the truth of the matter for others to decide. But today, I'm confident in telling listeners that the Righteous Among Nations in this scenario is Duckwitz, mainly because he's been honored as such by Yad Vashem.

There's also ample proof that Best played a double game by lying to Hitler that Denmark had become *judenfrei* during his command, making it hard to believe him when he said he was the one who warned the Danish authorities about the coming arrest and thereby enabling the great majority of Jews to go into hiding. For those in my audience who like to engage in hermeneutics – looking for the hidden meaning in a text – I mention Best's report to Berlin that the goal of cleansing Denmark of its Jews had been achieved. Semantically speaking, one could say because almost all Jews were now safely in Sweden, Denmark was free of them, but this claim disregards the linguistic or contextual nuances. Nor does it consider that Best could have been blatantly lying, for reasons we can only speculate about.

Now, decades after the war, credible evidence exists that Duckwitz was the one who passed word to the ousted head of the Social Democratic Party, who then informed the head of the Jewish community. As we saw earlier, Rabbi Melchior also had advance notice of the roundup when he told his congregation to go directly home from Rosh Hoshana services and into hiding. Additionally, we know Duckwitz had directly but secretly supported the Danish underground from the early days of the occupation. On the other hand, some sources claim he got his information from Best, so, if finally proven, it could weaken the claims of Duckwitz.

Today, I see a definite trend among those who show an interest in my Danish stories. I imagine it's because of erroneous information in the book Exodus and the film based on it, that so many are anxious to tell, rather than ask, me about an outdated conviction of theirs, that the Danish king wore the Yellow Star in loyalty to the Jews. They now know the old information isn't true, and they just want to share. *And, what do I have to say to that?*

"The old story was a real goodwill *coup*," I say for a start. "It did good for Denmark's reputation. As we know from Edward Bernays, and even from Ambassador Kauffmann's records, sometimes it's all in the perception."

And then I proceed to share the story behind another book that obscures the truth behind the so-called Miracle of Denmark: this one, a colorful children's book published at the dawn of the new millennium. Written by a Cuban-American writer, Carmen Agra Deedy, *The Yellow Star: The Legend of King Christian X of Denmark* is replete with vibrant drawings and a catchy narrative, pulling me right back into the subject of the Danish king riding his horse through the streets of the capital. Stout Danes fulfill my own childhood image of a happy people, although I didn't come face-to-face with a Dane until I went to Copenhagen on our 8th-grade class trip. Among vivid depictions in the book of mischievous children and playful Great Dane-dogs, I recognize the art museum *Glyptoteket*; most Scandinavians of my generation know of its history as the Carlsberg Brewery.

But then there's the Star of David. The tale has King Christian X telling his people that he expects every loyal citizen to follow his example. Soon the capital is filled with Danes, whom the award-winning writer calls "ordinary," as if there's such a thing, going about their daily business dressed in star-bedecked armbands. Another page of the book has the royal head defying the German sentry who's about to hoist the Nazi flag on top of the castle.

"If you do that," the king is quoted as saying. "One of our soldiers will remove it at once."

When the Nazi says the soldier will be shot, the king answers, "That soldier is I."

It's not until the back of the book when I notice the story specifically states it's a legend and probably not true at all. In a newspaper interview with the author I read she spent two years looking for proof that the story about the king actually happened. And then she concludes, it's "unverifiable." For publishing the story as is, she's been criticized by some although her usage of "legend" in the title should immediately alert readers that she's written a myth, like a timeless fairytale.

Maybe there's more credulity to the tale about the king and the Nazi flag which is flying over the most famous hotel, *d'Angleterre* (built in 1755 on the central square of Copenhagen), quickly claimed by the German military for itself. In this variation of the flag-on-the-royal-castle, the king still shows his defiance against the Nazi occupiers, leaving us once again to decide what we want to believe about the wartime situation in Denmark.

A F i n n i s h M a s s a g e

When I'm in a social group of Jews chatting about Scandinavia, the topic often veers to how their coreligionists are faring today. And then someone is likely to say something perfunctory to me about the Jewish community in Finland while, at the same time, admitting they don't know much about the past or current situation.

"You'll have to tell us more," they often say. And I nod and tell them that since my "husband's" passing (*will I ever be self-confident enough to stop this lie of marriage to Andy*), the large library of Holocaust-related books he left me has been my inspiration to dig deeper myself. It's like a voice from the grave, I say, telling me to develop my new knowledge into the broad Scandinavian presentations I now give at different venues in S. Florida. I don't tell them, if Andy were still alive I probably wouldn't have gone down that path because my life then would've been inextricably tied to the management of his OCD. Nor do I tell them that because I didn't want to appear ignorant before his father (I don't extend the lying to "father-in-law"), I got my early start to the Finnish experience through him.

Now faced with questions about the Jewish-Finnish situation during WWII, I'm stuck in the old insecurities. How can I possibly think I'm qualified to do justice to the individual actors in wartime Finland – the very human interest stories that so intrigue me – when the eminent historian and Nazi hunter Efraim Zuroff of the Wiesenthal Center in Jerusalem said not a word about my native country at a Miami forum on Scandinavia and the Jews? Asking him "why" made sense to me then but, still, I hadn't expected a tentative response from such a renowned scholar. "Finland was unique," he said. "It wasn't like the other Scandinavian countries...," his voice trailing off, leaving me to read whatever I wanted into that observation. But if he didn't know how to sum up this Nordic nation, could I really expect my listeners to be satisfied with my take on a very complex and serious topic?

At my next event, as the screen of my PowerPoint presentation illuminates the darkened room where I'm talking before mostly mature, life-long learners as opposed to a room full of active academics, I sense I have their full attention when I point to the pictures of a stout man hovering close to Himmler. "Who's this hat-less, smiling man in his pale trench coat joining the notorious SS Commander during two visits to Finland in 1942? Why the slide with both of them together?"

Nobody has an answer.

"Felix Kersten was his name," I say, still half-heartedly hoping for someone to nod with recognition. But they're all looking at me without a word, so I go on.

In brief, beginning in the spring of 1939, this man was Himmler's personal massage therapist, one of those jovial personalities who's generally easy to talk about, although the personal details behind this portly man are like many wartime stories, hard to verify. As we know, memoirs can't always be depended on for accurate recollections of historical facts because writers often paint themselves in the most positive light, unknowingly or for deliberate reasons of personal gratification.

The two penned versions of his memoir, one right after the war and another ten years later, only add to the mystique and intrigue of his story. His choice of words was probably influenced by his wish for a post-war citizenship in Sweden (as I mentioned before, his petition wasn't granted until 1953, after quite a lively debate in the Swedish Parliament). The self-important claims of having saved the Jews of Finland and the Dutch people also detract from his credibility and makes the choice of source material quite difficult. But still, just like with the other Finnish Holocaust-related person (Walter Cohen, to follow), who puts a human face on the fate of the Finnish Jews while he leaves a controversial legacy, Kersten must be included to round out the topic.

We know he was born in Estonia, then a Russian possession, from where he came to Finland, also part of the Czar's empire, to fight with the Germans in the Finnish Civil War (ended in 1918). That's where he became a second lieutenant in the army and was given Finnish citizenship. While recuperating in a military hospital in Helsinki, he was told by his doctor that he had the perfect hands for massage therapy, so he decided to get a certificate in the science of it. After the Finnish validation of his skills, he moved to Berlin to continue his studies with a famous Chinese masseur with an unverified doctorate. Later, Kersten, too, would claim the title of "doctor" due to a peculiar Finnish study system that, in the German tradition, rewarded a deserving medically trained person (in this case, a physiotherapist) with the highest title of *Medizinalrat* (only three such instances recorded in the Finland's history). There's no corresponding word in English although one source uses "medical counsel," which those of us who know the languages and culture involved, must reject as not quite precise.

Although his critics called him a *quasi*-medic, he continued to operate as a medical doctor with his therapeutic reputation spreading from Berlin to such notables as Queen Wilhelmina of the Netherlands who asked him to come treat her husband, the prince consort. Another grateful patient was Mussolini's son-in-law, the Italian Foreign Minister Count Ciano.

When he was appointed royal physician in the Netherlands, he took up residence at the Hague, which he found especially pleasing due to his Dutch ancestry dating to the 16th century. It was there that he got a call from Himmler about his stomach pains. The Reichsführer had learned about the success of the "Man with the Magic Hands" treating other influential persons, and now he wanted the therapist to himself. Kersten says in his memoir he first refused to relocate from the Hague, but then became afraid to turn down the most important Nazi after Hitler, because of implied threats to his safety.

He found the pale, infamous Reichsführer writhing in pain from intestinal spasms and colic, a condition worsened with stress. In his papers, Kersten also describes the leader of the SS as "narrow-chested, weak chinned, spectacled" and having a high-pitched voice. Soon, he wanted the doctor close by during all his travels through the Nazi-occupied territories. And Finland. "And" is an important conjunction used as a contrast, because – although I said it earlier, it remains a worthwhile repeat – the nation was never under German occupation. It was, however, the country of Kersten, a naturalized citizen, so it made sense from several standpoints that he accompany his employer there. In addition to keeping his patient fit, he could serve as a translator, and he could also share inside information with the Finns. Although he was never directly asked to be a spy for the Finnish government, Kersten was probably thinking ahead to post-war times when it would be important, maybe even a matter of life and death, to be on the winning side.

In March of 1942, the duo arrived in an unusually freezing Helsinki just two months after the *Wannsee* Conference, where the Final Solution as conceived by Eichmann had been adopted. Although Himmler had requested to travel incognito, mainly to inspect German troops and joint military sites in northern Finland, the Finnish hosts greeted him with all the state and military pomp a formal state visit calls for. It was, after all, the first time a Nazi leader of his importance visited Finland. Still, maybe because the March visit was billed as "unofficial," there was little written about it. His second visit, which lasted a total of three weeks in July-August, gave rise to much guessing that a roundup of the Jews in Finland was imminent. Adding more to the rumor was also Hitler's surprise drop-in at General Mannerheim's 75th birthday on June 4, which fell between the two visits of Himmler's in the same year.

Just like during his earlier visit, the Reichsführer again asked to travel incognito. In retrospect, this seems a laughable request since he had a prominent face, known throughout the territory. The Finnish State Police simply took surreptitious notice of his movements (with Kersten at his side), noting among all how he strolled the shopping streets of Helsinki and made small personal purchases, including loaves of bread. While the German News Agency did report on his meetings with both the President of Finland and Marshall

Mannerheim, it kept silent about his visits to the countryside. Kersten, who went everywhere with his employer, was officially referred to as the Reichsführer's "Medizinalrat." Later, detractors were less kind with their descriptions of him as a manipulator, even calling him the Devil's Doctor.

As the Danish Jews believed, death invariably followed in the footsteps of Himmler, but in the case of Finland the rumor mill was additionally fed by speculations about the peculiarity of the Jewish Question of that country. Some post-war writings have the Reichsführer telling the prime minister it was "shameful" Finland had had to accept Jewish refugees from Austria, and he even promised to have them sent back. The Minister is quoted as telling his visitor that the Jews were respected citizens who served in the army just like other Finns. Then, he put an end to any remaining discussion about the Jews by saying, "There's no Jewish Question in Finland."

The case of Himmler's Austrian Jews seeking refuge in Finland reminds me, albeit in a much smaller scope, of the MS St. Louis. The *Anschluss* had already taken place in March of 1938, and *Kristallnacht* was still three months away, when the Finnish ship *S/S Ariadne* arrived in Helsinki in August of that year, with 50 refugees from Austria. The Finnish consul in Vienna was then the only Scandinavian consular official still issuing visas to fleeing Jews, although at that time Finland had no official immigration policy. Puzzled officials at the port of Helsinki simply agreed there were no rules against admitting these refugees, so each received their coveted residency permit. But a week later, when the same ship returned with a load of 60 more Jews, it had to turn around.

History now tells us that refugees generally didn't seek to permanently settle in Finland but, instead, continued to look at it as a springboard to neutral Sweden. By 1941, the Swedes closed their doors to all Jews coming from Finland, and a year later, Swedish officials stated that admission of these refugees would be a sign of weakness unless, as they told the World Jewish Council in Stockholm, their "situation worsens." When Hitler's army was defeated in Stalingrad (1943) and with politicians believing the war would soon end, the Swedish approach to the situation was then expressed as "no longer necessary" (to admit the Jewish refugees waiting in Finland). The same year, the Swedes refused entry to 14 Jewish children from Finland, justifying their decision with saying the country didn't want "an invasion." At the same time, the government was in negotiations to admit 20,000 children from Belgium and France heading for Palestine. Records show officials were motivated by the good propaganda derived from keeping that plan alive. It wasn't until 1944 that 100 adults and children from Finland were finally allowed to enter Sweden, where they either settled or applied for their visas to America.

As we know, numbers and other facts don't always reflect the human side behind them. I find it particularly interesting that there were three groups in Finland standing in the way of any broader admittance of Jewish refugees to their country. The high numbers of unemployment followed by a shortage of food were given as reasons by the labor unions and the Social Democrat party, but perhaps surprisingly, the Jewish congregation in Helsinki was also opposed to the entry of more Jews. Several sources have guessed on the reason for this, something that wasn't unique to Finland (it also occurred in America): the fear of growing antisemitism following a large influx of Jewish arrivals. While open antisemitic expression wasn't common among the Finnish population, the bias of an official like the Chief of the State Police has been mentioned as a reason for the denial of some entry permits in addition to the deportation of some stateless Jews.

Today, as I read the different recollections from this period of Finnish history, I struggle with what to share and what to disregard as a post-war myth. For instance, the mystery with Himmler's black briefcase is an exciting story but who knows if it really is true. It seems he carried with him a complete list of all Finnish Jews, but the purpose of this information, which was easily attained through public records at any case, has not been explained. The storytellers simply speak of how agents of the Finnish State Police entered Himmler's Helsinki hotel room where they managed to take pictures of the contents of the briefcase, including the "list" that nobody else has seen. Even scholarly publications around the world later picked up this story to use as an argument that the Nazis planned to drag Finland through a Holocaust. Nobody has proven this theory to be true.

In his memoirs (the first one published in 1947), Kersten – the physiotherapist who never left the side of Himmler – doesn't mention the Reichsführer carrying any kind of list of all the Finnish Jews but, instead, boasts about a plan he (Kersten himself) put together with the Foreign Minister of Finland to spare their lives. The story falls apart when he writes how he'd left a sick Himmler in the hotel for a meeting with the Minister. Since the Nazi visitor was under constant surveillance by the Finnish State Police, who kept a detailed record of his activities, and there's not one mention of Himmler being ill then, the credibility of his therapist crumbles. Regardless, after the war, the Government of Finland awarded him a medal for "protecting" the Finnish Jews. The Netherlands took this honor one step further. First, that government gave him a medal for the positive influence he had on his prominent patient, which ostensibly had led to the cancellation of plans for a mass deportation of the Dutch people to Nazi-controlled lands in Eastern Europe and helped save national treasures from destruction. Second, the Dutch nominated him for the Nobel Peace Prize. Nine times, all futile. The French sought to join the chorus of accolades by awarding Kersten their Legion of Honor in 1960, but on his way to the ceremony he got sick, and three days later – ironically, while passing through Germany – he was dead.

It's a fact, of course, WWII was coming to an end in the spring of 1945. Not shy about his accomplishments in this period or any other time during his Nazi employment, Kersten also took full credit for having influenced Himmler to disregard the Führer's instructions to exterminate all remaining camp inmates, and to treat surviving Jews as POWs. His post-war memoirs (or "diaries," as he calls them) say he thereby saved tens of thousands of Jews. But when this hyperbole extends to his role in the famous Swedish rescue operation with the White Buses, one can't just dismiss this as bravado without a reminder of the previously told mission led by Count Folke Bernadotte.

As historians and others continue to ponder Kersten's role on the Holocaust stage, some people believe he was the original character model for Hitler's barber in a 1971 satire (the *Schmeed Memoirs*) by the great comedian and playwright of international repute, Woody Allen. Although both the coiffeur and the Finnish masseur tended to the personal needs of the two top Nazis – Hitler and Himmler, respectively – I don't see an obvious comic link between them. Then again, my trigger points for comedy may not be the same as Woody's.

By now, it's clear that any mention of a colorful individual like Felix Kersten (and for that matter, Walter Cohen, whose role on the Finnish war stage will be discussed next) leads to a variety of differing views of how he and other figures contributed, or not, to the survival of Jews in Scandinavia. The pieces of the puzzle I've chosen to share here don't claim to paint complete pictures because the source material is, as I already indicated, often confusing or contradictory.

Hymns Across The Bay

As I immersed myself in increasingly deeper research, sometimes in four Scandinavian languages, one distinct flashback kept popping up. This takes me to quiet summer evenings at our seaside cottage when the stillness was sometimes broken only by the sound of hymns wafting from a missionary rest home across the bay. By letting their joyful voices ring out through the stillness of our coastal landscape, the guests unabashedly violated all social convention. My parents knew you mustn't draw attention to your presence by making noise like that. Wasn't it enough that we had to put up with visitors in our little summer village, who weren't of the "normal" Lutheran kind? The whole scene was more than disturbing to our peace; it remained suspect for a long time.

And then there were the whispers about a previous guest, gone before my parents chose this location for their summer cottage; the man with the strange name, "Dr. Cohen."

Although the doctor and his wife weren't among the regulars during the years I can remember, Walter Cohen became one of those persons who live on in local and national lore. Not just because he held a key position in the fate of the Jewish refugees who were sent from Finland to a certain death, but also because his name will forever be connected to the "postcard drama," which is an integral part of the Jewish story. Then, there's his personal journey from being a German-born Jew (as was his wife) to becoming a Christian convert. Or maybe not. As so much else involving this man, it's hard, maybe even impossible, to separate the facts from what Finnish Holocaust scholars so politely call (his) "fabrication." Even in the best-researched books the dates of events are sometimes inconsistent with each other (one example only: the impossibility of the postcard bearing the clue to the mysterious deportation drama was, according to one author, postmarked on the same day it arrived in Helsinki).

In his memoir, which he first penned in Swedish in 1947, Cohen describes a set of coincidences and circumstances that strains the credibility and gullibility of any reader when he tells how he and his wife got to Finland (by way of Holland, Belgium, and Sweden), a country in dire need of volunteer soldiers for the Winter War (1939-40) against the Soviets. Without the necessary papers, he was promptly jailed in the port city of Åbo where, he writes, the Finnish prison pastor befriended him in fluent German. Although Walter says he had no faith in what he describes as a "Jewish God" and he still believed it was a sin to convert to Christianity, he accepted a Christian Bible from the pastor. Like many sudden and unexpected conversion stories, this one has an element of mystery as the book miraculously fell from a shelf in the cell to the floor, where it inexplicably opened to a verse in Isaiah. Walter Cohen was now inspired to convert.

He was released from prison in March of 1940, and – again with the help of the preacher – was embraced by the Evangelical sect owning and managing the rest home near our summer cottage. Now, it was too late to volunteer for the just-concluded Winter War (some officials are quoted as saying he wasn't fit to be a soldier at any case, although he claims service was the reason for going to Finland in the first place), so Walter settled in to practice medicine in the small town of Jakobstad, less than 10 miles from our cottage. Even when he was fined for practicing medicine without a license, his patients continued to love him.

As I said earlier, peace didn't come easily to Finland. Just as the Winter War was over, another deadlier war was soon to begin: the so-called Continuation

War against the Soviets, 1941-1944, where the Finns aligned with Hitler's soldiers against the common enemy. Since wartime regulations mandated that all able-bodied men between the age of 18 and 60 be drafted for the defense of the country, this included Cohen. He was sent to a brigade working on border fortification in the north where all Finnish soldiers, including anyone of Jewish faith, were separated by barbed wire from their German *Waffenbrüder*. Living conditions in these camps were tough, further deteriorating through a lack of food caused by crops ruined in the unusually harsh winter of 1942, and only somewhat alleviated when Germany shipped food supplies. Still, no scholar has ever compared the condition of the draftees with that in the Nazi concentration camps. Only Cohen did. While it's not possible to draw a direct line to his assertions that he lived in such a camp, the Swedish press then began using his description for the Finnish work camps.

For a moment overlooking the fact that he wrote in great detail about his conversion to Christianity, Walter had a dilemma when his first child, a boy, was born in 1941. Jewish tradition requires circumcision on the eighth day, but there was no *mohel* (circumciser) in Jakobstad, so he had to ask the Jewish congregation in Helsinki to send one. This inconsistency in his faith-based preferences (was he a Jew or a Christian?) isn't covered anywhere in his writing, but it seems to cast doubt on the sincerity of his conversion. Also, while sticking closely to his chosen script, he made reference to the 40 "other [sic!] Jews" when he bitterly complained about the standard conditions of the assigned work camp. Then there's the memorandum he wrote to the state police agency charged with alien matters, where he demanded that the "Jewish problem" be taken up by Parliament.

He also says he directed a slew of questions to government officials: "If we're not in a concentration camp, why can't we write home? Why don't we get furlough passes? Why can't we move around freely? Why aren't military doctors allowed to put us on sick leave?" But, what he doesn't discuss is how he, while a self-proclaimed concentration camp inmate, managed to file an application for Finnish citizenship (although unsuccessful).

The above activities, which also included Cohen's unauthorized leaves from the camp and self-initiated visits to high governmental officials in Helsinki, now set the stage for the disastrous consequences for a small group of Jewish refugees. With Cohen brushing over the outcome while crediting himself for saving himself and his family, I turn to other sources than his memoir for more facts on this suspenseful story with the tragic outcome for some of his fellow Jews.

The drama begins in July, 1942 with the move of Walter's labor group from their northern camp, where German soldiers were close by, to a garrison on an isolated island in the middle of the gulf between Finland and Estonia (then, Soviet-occupied). A major part of the work assignment consisted of twisting pieces of metal for the barbed wire, a task that often resulted in bloodied hands. If housing hadn't been to draftee Cohen's liking in the north, it was worse at this place where rats scurried around Soviet corpses buried under the wooden floors of the barracks. And antisemitic expression by some Finnish sergeants certainly made life harder for the Jewish workers than their gentile comrades.

When Cohen received a work furlough he hopped on the island ferry on its regular route to the closest Finnish port city (*Kotka*) on the mainland, where he continued by train to Helsinki, allegedly to plead for the closing of the camps. Overextending his leave, he then moved into a hotel frequented by prominent state officials. From there he continued to visit and write to people in high power. This is when he did the most damage to the Jewish refugee cause, with at least one Holocaust scholar believing his acts of defiance led the government to begin its aggressive pursuit of the expulsion of all persons without a residence permit. Although Jews were never separated on the lists of deportees, we know that among a group of 24 prisoners slated for deportation on August 26, 1942, there were five Jews; the others mainly Soviet POWs.

To be sure of the legal validity of the deportation plans, the officials involved with the case asked for an opinion of legal counsel to the Finnish Foreign Ministry who was an expert in international law. The matter seemed settled when he advised them asylum was a domestic matter of each independent nation and, therefore, Finland was in its full right to decide the case of Walter Cohen and the two other Jewish adult males on the deportation list. Later, this same lawyer was to become my professor in international law at the

University of Helsinki, where he refused to sign a letter of recommendation to the Hague Academy for me, because he'd already done it for three – as he emphasized by his voice – *male* students. It gives me great satisfaction to have recalled earlier in this book that his kind of gender bias didn't prevent me from being the only representative from Finland that fateful summer of 1967 at the Hague.

We now return to Walter's hotel in Helsinki, where on the evening of his arrest, the brother of the sitting President of Finland became a witness to Cohen throwing himself on the floor, kicking and screaming while demanding the right to speak with Marshall Mannerheim's representative. He also invoked the name of the Minister of Social Affairs, whom he had befriended in Jakobstad. It was all in vain. The State Police had had enough of Cohen, and he was returned to his assigned work detail on the island, where he'd remain for almost three months.

On October 27 (still 1942), Walter and eight other inmates were told to board a second boat for transport back to Helsinki. Since this was docked alongside the regular ferry handling traffic to the mainland, there was some speculation among the passengers, including Cohen himself, that the reason for sending the other craft was to keep the transport of the men from being seen by the public, who might have become outraged when they learned about the impending deportation. Regardless, even without an explanation for the dispatch of the second vessel, the nine were put on it, manned by only one machinist and a deckhand.

Somehow, the lone sailor overheard talk that Cohen was a physician who mistakenly had been placed in the labor service. On the way across the waters, this man motioned to Walter to step aside so he could privately ask for a prescription for what some sources imagine was a form of STD. The un-named sailor explained he couldn't make the request to the regular, regimental doctor for fear that this would mean hospitalization and a missed Christmas furlough.

Cohen, according to his own version, happily complied. Although this may leave us wondering why he carried a prescription pad under circumstances like that, nobody seems to question the veracity of what happened next as he pulled out a postcard from his pocket. On it, he wrote two lines, affixed a stamp and asked the deckhand to return the favor of the prescription by dropping the card in a mailbox. Addressed to Abraham Stiller, a leader of the Jewish congregation in Helsinki, the unsigned card reached its destination with the early morning mail on Friday, October 30. Later, Stiller would say he recognized the handwriting as that of Cohen, and the meaning of the cryptic message was unquestionable. Eternalized on a photograph in several publications, the two lines in Swedish are still indisputably clear. In translation, they say, *Nine men today to Bangatan* (street where the HQ of the State Police was located and where the nine inmates, including Walter, were awaiting their expulsion from the country), *hope you can meet us*.

Although Cohen didn't associate with fellow Jews, and he had a particularly particularly acrimonious relationship with Stiller, this compassionate and well-respected man with great connections to politicians and high government officials sprang into action. At that time, offices (and schools, for that matter) were open on Saturdays, which was an extra hurdle for Stiller, a deeply religious man with a sincere commitment to the observance of Shabbat. What he didn't know then was that the two government officials with sole authority over Cohen's arrest – the Minister of Interior and the Chief of the State Police – had already left for a weekend elk-hunt. Even a possible appeal on Saturday was out of the question, not only because it'd compromise Stiller's religion. Also, the two officials had been so confident of the outcome of the plan for deportation that a message had prematurely gone out the same day to the Gestapo chief in Tallinn that 27 illegal aliens were already on the ship to Estonia. The official list consisted mainly of non-Jews, a fact that historians use to support their argument that there was no racial policy applied to the selection of deportees. Nor were any of them citizens of Finland.

Meanwhile, Cohen remained in the jail cell where he (this is again his version of events) wasn't allowed to get his Bible from the stored-away luggage, as a guard told him there was "no need for it." The plan was for the inmates, which by then included Walter's wife and one-year old son, to be shipped out at 5 am the following Friday. Cohen, who sometimes shows great talent for details, noted there were 26 loaves of bread and two bottles of milk laid out on a bench, obviously as fare for the soon-to-be deportees. In addition to his own son, the group included another baby boy who, according to police records, was a "volunteer" for transport with his parents, the Georg Kollmans.

In his memoir, Cohen fails to explain how he managed to fall asleep clutching the Bible which apparently had been withheld from him. When he woke up that morning of November 6, 1942, the scheduled departure time of the *S/S Hohenhorn* had already passed. He doesn't write about the fate of the eight Jews who were on the ship on their way to Tallinn in Nazi-occupied Estonia, but we know from other sources that a trip that normally would take only a few hours took two days, due to the risk of mines-infested waters. Spending 10-12 days in the clutches of the Gestapo, the group of eight eventually reached Auschwitz-Birkenau where all but one person perished.

The lone survivor, Georg Kollman, born in Vienna, eventually settled in Israel. A physician by profession, he knew about Nazi experimentation with humans and he was determined not to participate in it, so he kept his medical training a secret in the camp. Instead, he was made to work in the coal mines. After he was liberated, he returned to Finland to testify in the 1947 post-war trial of the Chief of the State Police, who, as we recall, was one of the officials responsible for the deportation decision. Amazingly, Kollman appeared for the *defense*. When challenged by his fellow Jews about his statements in the official court records (a sentence "as light as possible," and "no desire for revenge"), he said, "Either way, I can't get my wife and child back." There's been much speculation on his motivation for acting in this manner of forgiveness and acceptance. He, himself, refused to elaborate, then or later (in 1979) when he was contacted by a Finnish journalist in Israel, where he lived till he died in 1992.

Returning to Cohen, who'd just realized he managed to escape deportation, I read how he claims it took him ten months to understand the success of the postcard. He also expressed his "joy" (his choice of words in the 1947 version of his memoir) over once again being sent back to the island camp, while his wife and son waited out the war in their home in Jakobstad. Later, he was relocated to work on a state-owned farm in the middle of Finland until the State Police decided he needed to be in isolation for all his propaganda activities.

After being jailed for less than three months (a "wonderful" time, as he writes), he was finally sent home to his wife. Less than a year later, in 1943, he was admitted to Sweden, having received his entry permit at least one year before other Jewish refugees in Finland (probably due to the friendship he'd cultivated with the Swedish ambassador in Helsinki). Then, the narrative gets fuzzy again.

According to Walter, he and his wife became missionaries at a hospital in Ethiopia, but other sources say this had nothing to do with evangelical fervor. Haile Selassie, the returning Emperor, had asked the WHO (World Health Organization) for medical personnel from neutral nations such as Sweden to build a health care system for his country, and the Cohens were happy to comply. After working in Ethiopia, the family returned to Sweden, where Walter died of a heart attack in 1957. His wife and son (and two other children, depending on the source one believes) left the one country that had finally taken them in, for sunny California where his wife passed away in 2005.

Although Walter didn't claim so himself, at least not publicly, his family lore has it that his postcard led to the interception of another transport ship and 150 lives were saved because of that. As research into the Jewish Question of Finland intensifies (and previously inaccessible wartime material is made available), new information on Walter Cohen continues to appear. It now seems unquestionable that he never became a licensed physician in Finland, and one source says that the Jewish Refugee Center in Antwerp, Belgium, contacted congregations in Sweden and Norway before he entered Finland, to urge them to prevent his entry into those countries. The director of the center even went so far as to say police should be called to arrest him on sight, because "he must have money in his possession." Unproven charges of embezzlement of funds and other illegal money matters were made at that time, while the accusation of a counterfeit passport and other documentation seems rather quaint today when one considers how this was the only way many Jews could save themselves.

When I read through the research-based books for additional details about Walter Cohen, I'm struck by the personal opinions of some of the writers. Descriptions like "unpleasant" and "egocentric" and that he showed "incredible overconfidence and rashness" compete with at least one conclusion that he "didn't conceal his hostility towards Finland and the Finnish authorities" (although at one point he claimed to have been born in Finland). These judgment calls, perhaps sometimes too hasty, make me think of how we must consider translated language through the prism of the prevailing culture at the time. Was it really overconfidence when Cohen tried to save himself and his family? Rashness? Hostility towards those very authorities who held his fate in their hands? Or, was it an unshakable will to live? Whatever the answers, and I have none, Walter Cohen survived.

M a s o n s   A n d   M a t i s s e

By now, I've developed a plan for how I speak about my Jewish-Scandinavian subject: either I talk about Denmark, Norway, Finland (in that order) with Sweden woven into the story about the other three or, I discuss the situation in my old home country as a separate session. Invariably, I'm surprised by something unexpected in the Q&A part, and then I get instant flashbacks to feeling unintelligent and uneducated when not knowing an answer to something. Today, the hours I spend on my constantly growing library show an almost obsession-like dedication (*am I channeling Andy*?) to the subject.

So what am I to do now with the elderly woman with her tailored suit and beautifully groomed hair, who raises her hand after one of my talks about Finland?

"Is it true that Sibelius was an antisemite?" Her earnest look suggests she isn't about to settle for an ambiguous response.

"Excuse me?" I say. Had I perhaps misheard her?

"I've heard how the Nazis admired him and that he was a member of some fascist organization, like the Freemasons. What do you know about that?"

What Masons? What praise by the Nazis had I missed?

I simply must think of something else that'd capture her interest. Like the 1990 action-thriller movie *Die Hard 2*. Surely, all association between this popular film and Sibelius must seem far-fetched not only to her but everyone else in the audience. At first, I'd describe how it's Christmas Eve in Washington, D.C., and Bruce Willis, or rather the character he plays, has 58 minutes to stop terrorists from causing his wife's plane to crash. After a dramatic pause, I'll then tell my listeners several bars of Sibelius's *Finlandia* are played twice as the tension rises in the film. Surely, as everyone ponders the ending, they'll forget the woman's question and I can move on.

Or, I'll just say it's inconceivable that Finland's most famous and cherished composer, Jean Sibelius, could have been an antisemite. The man who aroused the world with such majestic musical compositions as *Finlandia* and the *Swan of Tuonela*, among other grand creations, couldn't possibly have had any kind of public opinion on Jews.

Or could he? Much has been written about his depression and alcoholism so it isn't difficult to picture him making pejorative statements when he was in one of his dark moods.

I may be imagining it, but suddenly it seems like my audience expects more than any invented script I can think of. There's no choice now. I have to come clean with the woman, so I tell her I don't know if Sibelius had been an antisemite. To explain my lack of directness, I'll just say I've never had that question before.

Afterwards, when the lecture is over, I decide I must get to the truth. For my own sake.

To begin with, I learn Sibelius (1865-1957) had indeed been a Freemason. This piece of information gives me an instant flashback to a 1998-visit to Finland when an old friend proudly told me and Andy that he, my Finnish friend, had just become a Mason.

"That's nice," I'd said in a bland voice that I hoped conveyed the socially appropriate enthusiasm over an association I knew nothing about. At the time, there was no follow-up of the subject.

Later, as Andy and I left Finland for Germany, where we stood still and somber at many Jewish memorials, he broke his previous silence in Heidelberg by abruptly saying, apropos nothing I recall, "That thing about the Freemasons and your Finnish friend. Wasn't that some secret organization the Nazis liked?" Since we, and everyone else we knew then, traveled without the benefit of access to the Web, there were no instant answers to the question.

Finally, back in Miami at a visit to the public library, I learned that while Freemasonry is a secret association it's *not* known as a fascist group. In fact, already in *Mein Kampf* (1925), Hitler called the group an instrument for the subversive activities of the Jews; Masons had even been executed or incarcerated as political prisoners in concentration camps. And before Propaganda Minister Goebbels convinced the Führer of the PR-value of hosting the 1936 Berlin Olympics, he'd condemned the international games as a tool of the Freemasons (and the Jews).

Still curious about my Finnish Freemason friend, I dug for more. The secret fraternal order arrived in Finland in the early 20th century when a group of Finnish emigrants to America returned to Helsinki, bringing with them the idea of a society they knew well from the new country. Not only did they hope to bring in Sibelius, now a world-famous composer, as an organist for their organizational chapter but they also waived his membership fee for the first year, hoping to entice him to compose music for them. Showing us a side that neither fits with the stoicism of his countrymen or the serene images of the bald-headed genius we usually see on pictures, he's known to have cursed over having to use a harmonium as opposed to the more expensive pipe organ. And when his compositions weren't executed in what he considered the correct way, he complained so relentlessly that his reputation as a "grumbler" (the word used in biographies) was undeniable. Still, all the lodges in Finland continue to use only his music.

If there's such a thing as a revolution by writing music for a nation (Finland) and feeling the oppression of the political power (Russia) controlling it, Sibelius might provide an illustrative example. In 1899, when he composed *Finlandia*, the homeland of this Swede-Finn was still under Czarist rule that wouldn't end until there was a Civil War concluding with Finnish independence in 1917. Till that time, the symphonic poem could only be performed under different names at a variety of changing musical venues. Today, *Finlandia* is often erroneously believed to be the national anthem of Finland; I count myself among those who, like Americans with our *God Bless America* (also not an anthem), shiver of emotion when I hear the words or the music by itself. Revolutionary leaders on the African continent may have felt the same way when they adopted *Finlandia* as the state song for their short-lived Republic of Biafra.

Since parts of the composer's personal journals, written in his native Swedish, were published in their original language in 2005 there have been many efforts to scrutinize them for further musical, political, or other clues to his personality, including any antisemitic expression. One researcher went so far as to count the exact number of words in *other* languages he used in these private documents, such as Finnish (of which there were only 61), trying to derive meaning from that finding alone. Sometimes Sibelius even turned to Russian, Latin, French, or German to pen a thought in such a pithy manner that it's not always easy to get his intent. But a 1911 entry in Swedish may hint at his attitude towards Jews; here he described three of them in a crowded train compartment with him as "smelling bad." Presumably, they were among the impoverished Russians who, like so many others at the time, were looking for a better life in Finland, although still under Czarist rule.

The antisemitic quandary grows when I read about how the Germans loved all of Sibelius's music, already pre-Hitler, often sharing his fascination with mythology or nationalism. In 1942, the Nazi Propaganda Minister Goebbels gave his blessing for the establishment of a Sibelius Society for the promotion of the Finn's music in the Reich. But when German devotees of the late Viennese composer Gustav Mahler sought to join this organization, they were refused membership because the Nazis believed the Austrian had been Jewish. One can only guess if this was the twisted Nazi way of protecting the name of the respected 77-year old Finnish composer from being "tainted" by even an indirect association with a Jew.

Like most of his generation, Sibelius was fluent in German and prized the Teutonic heritage of the Nordic countries. He visited the country of fellow composer Richard Wagner at least 30 times, sometimes to perform, sometimes to collect royalties due him. After 1931, he never returned. Two years later, when the Third Reich came into being, he was already 67; a fact that's prompted a Finnish scholar to remind us that during the time of Nazis, the composer was "an old man with shaky hands and a cataract in his eye who probably didn't know what the SS was."

A common instance cited in relation to Sibelius's assumed antisemitism is his granting of a 1942 interview to a German reporter visiting in his home in Finland. On its own, that piece reveals nothing about his feelings towards Jews. Instead, in one of his diary entries from that period, he called the racial laws in Germany "puerile," and on another page from 1943 he accused the Nazis of "bad social prejudices." These quotes are from scholarly translations, a treacherous undertaking in itself, regardless of topic or language, particularly when excerpts are taken from someone's private journal in the tongue of the writer's choosing. Paraphrasing done without due care can also imply social and political biases of the original author and the translator where none exists.

When I consider the historical complacency of the world over the rise of Hitler and, therefore, the fate of the Jews, I believe we should ask ourselves if it's right to expect more from Sibelius? Should his understanding of the Jewish Question in Finland have been so unmistakably explicit in his diaries, the journals where a private person normally doesn't give any thought to interpretations by others, that retrospective readers should later be able to hold him above reproach? These questions are more relevant than flimsy conclusions based on speculation.

But the father of *Finlandia*, isn't the only gentile personality who links to the Nordic story about the Holocaust years in a roundabout way. In one of my presentations before a group of only women I displayed a picture of Sonja Henie, the Olympic figure skater from Oslo, Norway. The reaction was as I had hoped.

"She isn't Jewish, is she?" someone immediately shouted out.

I shook my head and then proceeded to share how the first Sibelius question had awakened in me curiosity about how some Gentiles with a public platform acted during the Holocaust years in Scandinavia.

In Helsinki of the '50s and '60s, every little girl with a pair of ice skates dreamt of being the next Sonja Henie. Although these metal contraptions had to be hooked on to our clunky winter shoes with a turn-key that didn't always work, my sister and I twirled and jumped in our heavy "ski pants" from the Jewish *lafka* I mentioned before. In my fantasy I was wearing the same white boots and short skirt that our Norwegian heroine introduced to the world, while I looped and twisted in my imaginary, perfectly choreographed moves. We knew nothing about Sonja being on the cover of Time magazine in July 1939, just that she'd won Olympic golds and that she was a movie star in Hollywood.

Fast forward to 2002 and my visit in Oslo. In addition to Jon, my friend from the summer at the Hague, I now have another Norwegian friend, Ove, whom I know from Miami where he maintains a third home. A single man of substantial means, both inherited and self-generated, he wants to be my tour guide in his home town, just like I'd been in Miami.

Had I seen the famous *Vigeland* Sculpture Park yet? The Viking ships? The iconic ski jump in *Hollenkolmen*?

"Been to those places," I say. "How about the Sonja Henie Art Museum?"

I know Ove likes fine art because he'd proudly shown me the three original Edvard Munch paintings passed on to him from his late father, an avid collector. I also know the family had moved in the highest social circles, although Ove insists he's not interested in nurturing the old contacts.

"Sorry, I won't take you there," he says now. "You see, in 1968, my father and his friends turned down an invitation to the formal opening of Sonja's museum, and I want to respect their decision. I've never been there myself, and I won't go now." From the silence that followed, I realize this is where his hospitality to me ends.

But why? I don't feel good about pushing my kind friend into doing something he doesn't want to, but before I can find the socially acceptable words – we're speaking a mix of Norwegian and Swedish with each other, so convention demands careful choices – he offers me the use of his car.

"You're on your own on this one," he says with surprising directness. "But I think you should know how she kept a personally inscribed picture of Hitler on her grand piano, and when the Nazi occupiers saw this, they left her mansion alone."

Since I'd experienced bewildered amusement and a bit of resistance from some other Scandinavian friends to what they thought was an obsessive interest in "the Jewish topic," I'd been reluctant to talk with Ove about my evolving interest in the Norwegian Jewry, but now I share the only thing I know about Sonja and the Nazis: her official salute to the Führer during the 1936 Olympics in Berlin.

"That's not true at all!" Ove says. "Yes, our press condemned her for the Hitler salute, but that was at another event *before* the Olympics. What we hated her for was that, after the games, she went to a private lunch at the Führer's home where he gave her the photograph of himself with that long and warm personal inscription. And we all read about how she helped his Propaganda Minister get a copy of her first Hollywood movie. There's more…"

I think he pauses for effect, or maybe he's just had enough of the subject. But he goes on.

"While she was sitting pretty, safe as an American citizen in America and making millions as a Hollywood star, my father and his friends were risking their lives in the resistance right here. Naturally, they asked for monetary support from her and other wealthy Norwegians at home and abroad, anyone who loved their homeland. But she didn't give them one dollar, not even one *öre*. Maybe now you can understand why so many of us resented her when she came running back to Oslo in 1956 with her wealthy third husband. Now she wanted the prestige of being a serious art collector, but many of us were still holding a grudge so when the museum opened in 1968, we didn't go."

"But, the art must be worth seeing today?" My meek voice shows I don't know how to proceed with this topic since Ove gets quite emotional about anything relating to Sonja Henie. Somehow, in typical Scandinavian fashion, we manage to drop the subject without another word.

A year after her museum opened, on a flight from Paris to her home in the

Norwegian capital, Sonja Henie died. It seems the leukemia that killed her at the age of 57 was deadlier than the rancor among her countrymen over her lacking empathy for Norway's freedom fighters. In the end, she did acknowledge why some of them considered her a *quisling*, the Norwegian eponym for traitor.

In 2012, the Henie art gallery is major news in the Oslo papers. In a "first case in Norway" of Nazi-looted art, the heirs of a Paris art dealer want the return of the Matisse, *Blue Dress in a Yellow Armchair*, painted in 1937 and confiscated by the Nazis in 1941. After initially refusing to cooperate, museum officials relent in 2014. Rightful ownership is restored, and the painting returned to the lawful owners.

I've yet to see Sonja's collection.

"Is She Jewish?"

As a girl in Finland, I imagined myself aristocracy, which gave me a safe space in which to live the fantasy I was *not* the outcast I really was, but merely chosen for some superior purpose. Not even my American prince had been able to save me from being an outsider, first in the Deep South where we began our life together and, then, in Miami where we pursued our happily-ever-after that ended in divorce. It was in that heavily Jewish community where I first came face to face with a population showing me the possibility of something I'd only imagined before: a sense of connecting and belonging, of finally fitting in.

To this day, old friends and new acquaintances remain puzzled. What do I mean, they demand to know, when I say I found comfort in the Jewish community. This *shikse* in sheep's clothing whose birth religion, so history tells them, has condemned the Jews too many times. And they want me to know that, even now, there may be people in remote areas who've never seen a Jew and, therefore, believe the old tale of them growing horns like the devil himself. On the other end of the spectrum are Jews who are innately uncomfortable around a Gentile like me, one who spouts Yiddish expressions and laughs at Jewish jokes. How come, they ask, *you ..., you who didn't take that final step of conversion*?

The simple explanation, the one I keep repeating when I don't want to elaborate: Jews were the first to embrace me for who I really was, insecurities and all. It didn't matter if I was Scandinavian nobility or a Swedish- or Finnish-speaking Finn. With their questions, they then pushed me on the long road to discovery of the wartime fate of their Scandinavian compatriots.

Along the way came Andy, the OCDer and partly Yeshiva-educated atheist, to show me how good it is that history, even when it comes in its most evil, systemic, bureaucratic form, is kept alive. His legacy to me was that I, quite OCD-like myself, wasn't able to leave the subject alone. It began with my search for additional material, any of the four Nordic languages would do, and then, at some point, it evolved into my commitment to sharing my new-found knowledge wherever there was a group who wanted me.

Now with both feet in the middle of Jewish-Scandinavian history during WWII, I find it impossible to separate my past from Jewish culture where the familiar sense of humor and the enrichment of Yiddish expressions have added to my sense of fitting in. Somewhere I read that the old Jewish language, which some say is dying, is one of "irony and defiance" and then I understand its appeal. Surely, the rebellious Vikings had similar linguistic concepts, now fixed in the DNA of the Nordic people and found in their often-dry sense of humor. To survive, the Jews had to see the irony – the humor, if you will – in their often-tragic history, which shows us today how past generations persevered through stubborn self-reliance. Could it perhaps be that humor is deeper ingrained in Jewish culture than others? "Like being Finnish?" as a documentary on Jewish humor asked.

As an interviewee in that movie said, there are probably 100,000 books on being Jewish but no more than 100 on being Finnish. Obviously, one can't compare humor in a large culture to a much smaller one. Then he shared what he called a "funny rule" of Scrabble (at least on Facebook, where he's an avid player), where *jew* as a verb is accepted, but *Finn* is not because it's a proper noun that must be capitalized, which isn't permissible in the game. When I've shared this with Jewish friends, they laugh in spite of the underlying antisemitism, while Finns stare numbly at me.

Even without their humorous take on any given situation involving them, the way Jews in my social circles express themselves amazes me. For one thing, the noisiest disagreement with loved ones doesn't necessarily result in cutting someone out of the family circle, or at least not until there's a lively debate about it. Scenes of that nature make me cringe at the thought of the years in Finland when the list of my family's "unacceptables" was constantly shifting, making it impossible to know if it was permissible at any given time to talk with this or that relative. Further confusing me then was that there was no understandable reason; my mother or father, separately or together, would only hint at something unacceptable done by the shunned person.

The Jewish loyalty to family also shows itself in traditions. One friend told me her parents made sure to invite long-lost relatives to their Passover, including Jewish acquaintances without a direct relationship to the hosts, even non-Jews. This made me share with her how anyone dropping in on us in Helsinki on the second day of Christmas was promptly labeled a "Christmas swine," obviously an accusation of unacceptable holiday behavior. Since then, I must have developed better sensibilities when I offered my first seder invitation in Miami to a Jew. Although I acted out of silent deference (*how Scandinavian of me!*) to the hostess's space limitations, she'd have been justified in marking me ungrateful. Instead, she kindly explained the universal theme of her holiday, saying that was the time for people of all faiths to contemplate freedom from oppression.

Still, the conversion questions continue as if my welfare depends on how I answer them. With some parties it's a matter of religious or practical choice (*have you considered converting so you can join a temple?*), with others it's about personal genealogy (*have you checked your roots, maybe you're Jewish?*).

As I said earlier, I didn't come from a traditionally religious family. My mother (and hers), scoffed at anything even remotely invoking a deity, unless she needed a god to back her up in scolding me for not having been "nice" to her. For years afterwards, really decades later, when in a particularly dark mood, she'd drag out the shame she felt when my Kindergarten teacher told her I'd asked a question in class. *Imagine, thinking you're special! What a disgrace for a mother to hear that!*

On the other hand, my father, the teacher of Lutheranism and world religions, believed you didn't need churches to worship God. "He's all around us," he said. Particularly on Sunday mornings when he preferred to take me along on long walks instead of sitting on hard wooden benches in some sanctuary. As we say in Swedish, he was a "from" man, meaning he was devout in his own quiet way; some books call it being "warmly religious." This doesn't equal the Yiddish "frum" (both words pronounced the same way), which is used with really pious believers.

It'd take several years living in Miami, and it was the first time in my life, when I heard someone calling Luther an antisemite. And, I was mortified I came from a religious tradition whose leader despised Jews. But then, as life is filled with these inexplicable events that fit in with each other like a puzzle, a request landed on my desk: could I use the attached sermon by Rabbi Melchior of Copenhagen from September, 1943 as a starting point for "something in honor of the Danish rescue?" As I mentioned earlier, on the morning preceding the day of the scheduled roundup rabbi had urged his congregants to go directly home from the cancelled service so everyone could go into hiding. The rest of the real rescue story is also familiar from a previous chapter.

The big envelope, seemingly in my mail by accident, contained a proposed service that included the history of the arrival of the Jews into Denmark; 11 pages endorsed by the *National Conference on Christians and Jews*. There was also a suggestion for Americans to decorate their sanctuary with Danish-language signs, reminiscent of the Krystalgade Synagogue (built on land bought by the Jewish community in Denmark in 1799), and even to use blow-ups of the New York Times from September 30, October 1, 2, 3, and 4, 1943. All to commemorate the Danish rescue.

I contemplated all this as I looked at the letterhead from a New York organization called *Thanks to Scandinavia*, established in 1963 by Victor Borge and a friend as a vessel for scholarships to be distributed between America and the Scandinavian countries. After several meetings and brainstorming sessions with a local board member of the AJC (American Jewish Committee) and two Lutheran pastors, an open venue was finally found for a two-day ecumenical dialogue subject-lined "Luther and the Jews: Reflections on Kristallnacht and Anti-semitism." Although the wartime sermon at the synagogue in Copenhagen was an inspiration, the requested honor-the-Danish-rescuers-event it wasn't.

On the first day of the workshop-slash-seminar I saw the printed five-page program for the first time, and I cringed when I read the lines under the header, "A Difficult Subject." *How was it possible that all my religious (meaning Lutheran) classes in Finland never mentioned the vitriolic words now excerpted in black and white from Martin Luther's treatise "On the Jews and Their Lies?" How come I never heard my early Lutheran pastor in Miami talk about how the Reformer spoke of taking away all (Jewish) prayer books and Talmudic writings, and setting fire to synagogues and schools? What about Luther calling the Jews a "rejected and condemned people?"*

Was there atonement for me, somewhere?

In 1959, my father had written a small, uncritical text he called *Lutherord* (Luther's Words). Twenty years after his death, a stash of old things from before my law school days in Helsinki kept calling on my compulsive interest in the truth. Nervously curious about the nature of his selections – biased or balanced; perhaps casting aspersions on my father and, by association on me? – I located the small, purple-covered book with its fly-page inscribed by the father-author to his daughter, me.

With care that's more typical of a police detective, I scrutinized each page of the Swedish text for some sign of Luther's infamous antisemitic pronouncements, edited by my father for purposes of his thin book. I knew how easy it was to manipulate readers when using quotes, but I also knew the devil was in the facts, so I willed myself not to miss the tiniest detail in my father's chosen excerpts. Oh, the relief when I found only two paragraphs with a passing mention of the Jews! One excerpt had him saying if the apostles, all of them Jews, had "treated us heathens as we did the Jews," nobody would ever have converted. If he were a Jew himself, Luther said, he'd rather be a swine than a Christian when seeing how some "asses" (or, as the Swedish expression goes, heads of asses) lived their faith. Even the most critical eye must agree that Luther – in the version of my father, that is – showed some compassion for the

Jewish people of his time.

In the handout from the two-day gathering, I also read that in 1983 when the Lutheran Council in Stockholm celebrated the 500th anniversary of the Reformer's birth, it declared ("to their tardy credit," as the printed program so succinctly said) that "we cannot accept or condone the violent verbal attacks the Reformer made against the Jews." There was no mention of any conciliatory statements like in my father's booklet.

One year after I met Andy at that fateful Break-the-Fast, we'd been at Yom Kippur services in the synagogue where most of his friends attended, I sat self-consciously next to him (*nice, soft chairs*), apprehensive about the glances thrown my way because I was an obviously unknown entity in that congregation. Cautiously scanning my surroundings, I saw what I thought was a palpable lack of awe and reverence by most congregants. People kept coming and going, often not even muffling their voices to a muted whisper when they spotted someone they knew. The social chatter around us stopped me from quietly withdrawing to the prayer book that Andy handed me. Still, I was flush with warmth from sitting next to the man I loved, and the thought that the prayers on this particular High Holy Day formed a chain between Jews around the world was in itself inspirational. One couldn't say the same about Christian Good Friday services held by Baptists, for instance.

As the years went by, and from observing our Jewish and gentile friends, I became increasingly aware of how they differed in their approach to their religion, and I started wondering if I even could convert. I'd learned about my own faith as a mandatory, spoon-fed subject at school and being told in confirmation classes what "we" believed in, but now I saw how Jews *argued* even the smallest religious portion in their Torah-studies. And, if they didn't argue, they *questioned*. Not in a polite measured Scandinavian way, but often loudly, even raising their voices with their rabbi when they used Bible passages to support their own opinion.

The kind of Gentile I was frowned on infusing modern dilemmas with a scriptural quote. If Christian friends had talked about how Cain and Abel resolved their sibling rivalry, or volunteered their thoughts on the meaning of something in the Bible, I'd have thought they were going evangelical on me and feared they were "losing it." Still, the emotional challenge of letting go of one's religious heritage can't be overestimated. Even when I was quite removed geographically and emotionally from my parents, I didn't have the courage to face what I imagined would be their further condemnation of me as a person if I shared an intention to convert. But in fairness to them, they, or the fear of their disapproval, couldn't have been the sole reason why I didn't become a Jew-by-choice.

Having babies with Andy would perhaps have changed the outcome, but we were adults with offspring already creating their own lives. At this stage in my life, I reasoned with myself, the spiritual journey was mine alone, without consideration of anyone else, particularly a secular Jew like him. If he'd been a Mormon or Scientologist, conversion wouldn't even have entered my mind so what was it that made Judaism different for me now? But when I thought of the rich history and tradition, both evident in Jewish values and devotion to family, I knew I couldn't let go of the conversion dilemma so easily. Moreover, since the main religious questions, maybe even some considered insignificant, had been debated by such ancient sages and scholars like Hillel (whose name is on buildings at Jewish university campuses around the world), this had led to a belief system so solid that it's withstood centuries of challenges by believers. Surely, it'd leave nothing for me to doubt.

Earlier, I shared my first exposure to a side-by-side comparison of Judaism with Catholicism and Protestantism. My friend at the hosting synagogue then became my go-to reference on all things Jewish. But when I joined her and her family for Friday night services, I didn't have the same sentimental reaction as I still have during an Episcopal service with Holy Communion. Maybe it's the music. The old familiar choral presentations often make me teary and although I can't expect my favorite Swedish hymns to be sung at my funeral in Miami, I've made arrangements for my ashes to be interred at a local garden-like Episcopalian Columbarium. The picture of my sons sitting in quiet contemplation on the bench facing my chosen vault is quite comforting.

Early in our relationship, Andy brought back from Israel a necklace with my first name spelled in Hebrew letters, prompting my older son to ask, "Mom, are you turning Jewish?" At that time, we laughed over hasty conclusions based on jewelry alone, but now I look at that reaction as ignorant bewilderment by a young person. Today, I can't just laugh away the more serious questions coming my way when the complicated subject of antisemitism follows casual conversations about my conversion or non-conversion. Have I considered the expected antisemitism; do I know how to deal with that? And, perhaps more importantly, do I really want to make the Holocaust that personal?

There are, of course, countless theses on the definition of antisemitism but, for me, it's personal when people make offensive comments about Jews as a group. Usually, this happens when they assume I'm not part of it (*she doesn't look Jewish*), and somehow they are free to express their true feelings in words or body language. Like with an obscenity, when you hear or see it you feel the assault on your personhood. Here, a stranger on a tour bus in Los Angeles comes to mind.

Traveling solo shortly after Andy had passed away, I sat quietly in my seat on a Los Angeles sightseeing bus when a nondescript lady across the aisle began chatting me up in an obvious effort to find company for the rest of the day-long tour. Finally, she asked about the reason for my visit from Miami.

"Oh, I'm here as the parliamentarian for the NCJW," I said with the hope she'd leave me alone. Perhaps she'd find my position with the organization too daunting to pursue.

"What does that stand for…, *N-C-J*…?" she continued instead.

National Council of *Jewish* Women," I said. My tone came with a yellow light indicating that my personal judgment of her lack of worldly background was immediately to follow if she said anything about the Jewishness part.

But she didn't say another word and, instead, turned her back towards me. There was no doubt in my mind that her silent act was because she mentally identified me as a Jew.

In another instance, I was on a cruise with my new husband (yes, three years after Andy's death another Jewish man proposed marriage to me) where we were assigned a specific dining table for the duration. When we both agreed we didn't like the arrangement, I knew what to do.

The opening came when the other lady demanded to know the origin of "your accent," to which I said something evasive about Scandinavia. Her annoying tone when she said, "Obviously, you must be Lutheran" made me wink at my husband; Jewish, as he was but never as willing as me to poke a hole in preconceived beliefs by others. He wasn't surprised when I said, quite devious with a big smile, "Actually, I'm not. I belong to a small Scandinavian minority. I'm *Jewish*!"

After that, the table was ours alone.

The answer to the other conversion question (*did I really want to make the Holocaust that personal*?) takes a bit more effort on my part. How to explain in a non-lecturing tone, my journey towards a sense of fitting in that goes beyond loving a Jewish man like Andy with his increasingly obsessive interest in the Holocaust? In the wrong words, I may sound as if I'm so desensitized to the historical atrocities as to lack empathy for Jewish survivors. But shared in the right way, my knowledge about what happened to the Jews in Scandinavia during the Holocaust Years makes their fate both a matter of universal shame and triumph.

Serendipitously – there's that instructive episode in my life again! – I tuned in to a Zoom presentation by a female executive of a powerful multinational company just as I was putting the finishing touches on this book. The corporate message through her was that being inclusive doesn't equal belonging. At that moment, I understood that just because the Scandinavian society self-promotes as "inclusive" doesn't mean it is, or ever has been. Finally, I could accept the broader reason for why I hadn't felt like I belonged in my Finnish life and how this led to an ongoing search for a place to fit in. I had to leave home to find home.

But with age comes wisdom, and with it, the modification of any kind of simplification of early lessons. For me, an old essay by a Jewish-Hungarian camp survivor who settled in Sweden added needed perspective when he wrote of the Jewish mentality to accept reality as it is, making the best of it. How many times have I heard my Jewish friends say, "It is what it is" when faced with a scary or annoying situation? To that, I add my personal observation about the respect I receive from Jews who acknowledge who I am as a person, showing acceptance without any discernible judgment. Even when they tell their friends, "Well, she isn't Jewish."

My youthful survival tool had been to prepare myself for life as a princess, although not the Jewish-American kind of whom I knew nothing then. When I married my American prince he unwittingly fed into my delusion by praising me for being a "real lady." What I didn't realize in my life with Andy was how movie-like my life-long play-acting was. When I was swept along by the billow of romance that came with loving the first Jewish man I knew, I believed it was my destiny to be his Star, the Leading Lady, the Prima Donna in his life. At first, he was the producer of the new celluloid creation I was living. My future with him seemed so easy. I could make myself fit right into any new role. But then, without me noticing, he became the director with absolute control over the script and the budget.

When, in the foreshadowing of his mental disorder, the plot started to change on a daily basis, reality finally pierced a hole in the veil I wore in my dreamy love epic. Feelings of confusion and demoralization made me wish for more directives and clues to the true genre. Was this science fiction? A mystery where I had to wait to the end to see who the villain was? Or could it be that, all along, this was a documentary of me as woman gone blind? It wasn't until I did a full screening after he was gone, that I knew. It never mattered to him what role I played. From the first scene I was only one of his props.

A year after Andy's passing, I found the "script" he left behind. There, among the huge piles of Holocaust videos and books I had an awakening: while the Jewish narrative of WWII was a major part of his obsessions, his collection of material was now becoming a preoccupation of mine too. But where he and I differed, at least that's what I tell myself today, is in two instances: I read all my sources, and I freely share my knowledge with any audience that'll have me. Only in moments of harsh self-examination, when I struggle with containing loads of information on the Scandinavian wartime experiences, I tell the Andy who still resides within me that I must now be driven only by the space limitations of my current life.

"That's not the way a Northern star looks like," my first-grade teacher had said about my six-pointed star.

Although I never drew another star in class again, the allure of the cosmic lights continued at home. Still six-pointed, the celestial bodies were sparkling symbols of something mysterious, something comforting and even heroic. Everyone knew the Polar star guided sailors lost at sea, and how it hovered protectively right over our homeland, Finland, while the threat of the giant, next-door neighbor, the Soviet Union, continued to loom large in my mind.

As usual, I found comfort in books. My sister and I wore out the pages to the *Birch and the Star*, the classic Swedish-Finnish children's story set during one of the many wars that are part of our country's history. Written in 1893 by the legendary Zacharias Topelius (it's well into the new Millennium that I learn he came from one of the first Jewish-Finnish families), the doleful story centers around a brother and sister who're sent far away from famine and war, where their longing for home never stops. They know they'll be back at the old homestead when they see the evening star still beaming brightly through the branches of the tall, slender birch tree with its familiar spotted trunk. While my sister cried over the sorrowful prospect of the siblings being lost forever, my hope for a happy ending was never shattered. I knew about the shining star, I said, and didn't she understand how it always guided the children home to their waiting parents.

"That's not the way a Northern star looks like," my teacher had said.

Ten years after Andy's death I receive a package from Finland. In the odd mix of things carefully and individually wrapped in the Helsinki newspaper, I find a Swedish-language children's book, printed in Finland in 1948 and inscribed to me by my parents. Brumbo och stjärnorna (*Brumbo and the Stars*). As I flip through the colorful pages, looking at Brumbo the bear using the Sandman's umbrella for a journey through the Milky Way, I suddenly see it. No *them*, because the pages are loaded with six-pointed yellow stars. Six points that light up Brumbo's adventures when he visits the Man in the Moon and plays on the constellations of stars colorfully sprinkled throughout the book by the illustrator.

That's not the way a Northern star looks like.

But today, I know. Lopsided or not, with six or five points, "Jewish" or Northern; it no longer matters. They're all part of my universe.

9 Questions To Ponder Alone Or With Others

Did your overall impression (preconception) of the Jewish-Scandinavian wartime experience change after reading the book? How?

What does the writer mean when she says she looked at herself as the star in a movie?

What price, if any, did the writer pay for living a life of self-delusion? Was there any change or evolution in her; if so, what triggered it?

What motivates the writer to look for a sense of belonging in Jewish culture and tradition?

How does the writer struggle with conversion? Is there one specific thing that led her to a decision?

How is this part of Nordic history relevant to Americans today? To Jews?

Can the wartime experience in Scandinavia (in the four countries discussed, or in only selected ones) be used in teaching tolerance in today's world?

Do you think it's possible for non-Jews to *notice* and *feel* antisemitism in our society?

In 2016, Oxford Dictionaries selected *hygge*, a Nordic concept for a simple life, as a finalist for the Word of the Year. Do you see a connection between it and the ancient Scandinavian code of conduct (mentioned in the book; later called Jante's Law)?

Cami Ann Green

The Yellow Star that Wasn't

Acknowledgement

First and foremost, I want to acknowledge my long-time, best-ever writing friend, Nancy Kalikow Maxwell (author, *Typically Jewish*, University of Nebraska Press, 2019). She and I spare no words when critiquing each other, all in the spirit of pushing each other to that elusive end-product of "best we can do." For many years, we probably kept Einstein Brothers and Offerdahl's in business as we met to talk about the many glitches we discovered in each other's drafts.

The list of others who've influenced me in writing this particular book is long. Listing them in no specific order, I want to thank Annie Landau (astute book critic, not only mine), Andrea Pallin (who, hopefully, doesn't remember the first draft), Joan Worton (an old friend of Andy), Donna Silver and Carolyn Stein (both of whom have been at my "Jewish lectures"), Libby Murray (intrepid reader, always happy to listen to my stories), Fay Weiss (who showed me friendship between people of vastly different backgrounds can begin with a chance meeting), Donald Dewey (whose books and journal articles I fell in love with; did he really tell me to burn my first working title?). For fear of overlooking others by name, I take the coward's way out by thanking everybody else as a group.

I also offer my sincerest gratitude to every person who's ever been at one of my "Jewish presentations" where you challenged me with questions that ended up in my book, in one form or the other. This includes my two sons, Bothwell and Sam, whose comments and observations have often led me down a path I hadn't thought of before. Thanks to each and every one of you, I was inspired to broaden the subject.

In different ways, two husbands (my ex, the father of my sons, and my late spouse, Donald) were instrumental in shaping my journey through the subject. But without "Andy" in the book, I wouldn't even have gotten off to a start. Even though now long dead, he's the one person in my life who set me off on my obsessive path of finding the facts of what happened to the Jews in Scandinavia (many of whom were fortunate enough to have escaped from Hitler's claws) during the Holocaust Years.

To everyone above, and many more, I offer more than heartfelt thanks.

Cami Ann Green

Author Information

Cami Ann Green is an award-winning author of three human interest stories (*Tales2Inspire* anthology). Over many years, she's also filed pieces on her observations of life in America with several Scandinavian publications both in Finland and the US (including a face-to-face interview with Pulitzer Prize-winning novelist James Michener).

She holds two law degrees, and a PhD. Her professional career was as a law school administrator and university professor. Venues for her academic writing (under "Green" as well as "Hofstadter") range from two law reviews to her latest book on modern consuls (Palgrave Macmillan).

Today, she continues to give presentations on two of her favorite topics: Scandinavian Jews during WWII, and the nature of foreign consuls functioning in communities throughout America.

For more information, please go to her website: http://www.CHofstadter.com

CPSIA information can be obtained
at www.ICGtesting.com
Printed in the USA
BVHW090425161221
624023BV00013B/1275